I0445591

Tales of an Amish Taxi Driver

Book 1

My Journey into the

Amish World

Haley Straw

Disclaimer

This is a work of nonfiction. The Amish are God-fearing, humble, hardworking, and most strive to be good people. Many Amish I met expressed feeling blessed to be born into the Amish faith. They see it as a mission from God to stand as a light to a world replete with darkness.

Each person in the story is real; however, identifying details such as names and locations have been changed to protect individual privacy.

I did my best to accurately recreate conversations and events from my memories, to bring forth my experiences, and to accurately portray the Amish people and culture. The events described were real and shared from my point of view, as others involved may recall the events differently.

Copyright© 2021 by Haley Straw. All rights reserved.

ISBN - 9798999631909

Acknowledgments

I would like to express my deep gratitude to Ardyth, Lezlee, Nadine and Peggy for generously giving of their time and expertise to critique my work, and for their belief in me as an author

To the Amish for their open hearts and homes and for the memorable shared experiences; especially that of my dear friends Danny and Susie

To Eli and Daniel, Amish friends who have traveled many miles with me for reviewing the manuscript before publication to assure cultural accuracy and respect

And most importantly, to my six children; the ones who mean the most in my life. They shared in many of my adventures, and when they weren't along, held down the fort while I was away.

Author's Note

Returning home to Oregon after one year of driving the Amish in Missouri I was accosted by friends who were curious about the Amish people and culture. They wanted to know everything about the Amish and hung on my every word with rapt attention.

Why? What makes the Amish so intriguing to the outside world? I believe it can be summed up in one word; values. The Amish teach them and live what they profess to believe. The Amish have many beliefs, and as I've gotten to know them three main ones stand out to me.

Humility: you can see it in their simplicity of dress, the neatness of their homes, and the traditional way in which they travel.

Community: you can see that in how they serve and support one another in their close-knit society. When a building burns, funds are taken up and donated and free labor is given. When one falls ill meals are brought in, and chores are taken over by volunteer community members. When a large event such as a wedding or funeral is to happen everyone helps with cooking, cleaning and set up. Homes are freely opened to out of town guests.

Family: they trust God in his timing and the number of children given to the family. Mothers tend to the home and children while fathers and young men provide. Families work together, play together, study together and pray together. They take care of their own elderly and infirm instead of relegating that to outside sources. The Amish believe in so much more, which you'll find out in reading my subsequent books.

What is important in your life? Look closely at the lives of the Amish as you read through my stories. What similarities are there? What differences are there? Do you see anything they value that you could value more? What is it about the way you live your life that exemplifies that value? What changes can you make in your life so when others look at who you are, what you say, and what you do, they will see those values?

As you read my writings, I invite you to ask yourself, "What do I value? Can others see it by how I live my life?" If you truly value something you make it a priority in your life, as the Amish do.

Additional Note

While at lunch with my marketing man and his wife at the local barbeque joint, the topic came up of protecting those I was writing about. My concern was the characters in the book would be able to be identified and their privacy compromised. Matthew suggested I just tweak any identifying qualities of each of the characters, and then I remembered who I was writing about...the Amish. A trip I took to Wisconsin came to mind. I dropped Levi Otto off at an Amish estate auction. He asked me to return in four hours, find him; then we would go. Visions of three-hundred Amish men, including Levi, who had a bowl haircut and long beard just like everyone else, wore straw hat, black shoes, black suspenders and homemade dark slacks just like everyone else, and who had a solid color colored shirt on either a shade of blue, brown or green, just like everyone else. How would I find him in that sea of sameness? Yes, I described the Amish as they were, but it could be almost any Amish that I was describing. By the way, after walking around and around and around looking at dozens of Amish men faces and asking a few women along the way I finally did find Levi.

Contents

Disclaimer ii

Acknowledgments iii

Author's Note iv

Additional Note vi

1. Levi the Amish Guy 1

2. Misconceptions 5

3. First time in an Amish Home 9

4. Second Meeting 13

5. The Beginning 19

6. Becoming Official 25

7. First call to Haul 29

8. First Day of Hauling 33

9. A Christmas unlike any other 37

10. Feeling Famous 43

11. Home Again 51

12. Visit to the Dentist 57

13. Acceptance 63

14. The Rural Bus Driver's Trip to 67
the Chiropractor

15. Driving Someone New 75

16. A Wild Nights Drive...79

17. The Amish are Human too................................85

18. Driving the Business.......................................95

19. Mad Bull..105

20. Directionally Challenged...............................117

21. Thanksgiving Rush.......................................123

22. Doggonit! 133

23. Surprise Visitor 139

24. Trailer Troubles 145

25. Samuel Shetler from Helena, Missouri.....155

26. Salt and Pepper 165

For Further Information...II

Upcoming Book Two IV

Amish Christmas Mishaps IV

About the Author VII

1

Levi the Amish Guy

The Amish and I became acquainted about three years ago. My husband and I, along with our six young children, left the bustling, progressive West Coast of the United States to settle in the slower paced, primarily traditional-valued Mid-West. We were blessed to pay cash for our home, however; it wasn't suitable for human habitation when purchased. The home had an outdated heating system, broken windows, missing doors, missing woodwork, and a missing bathroom sink. Adding to that, the whole house, floor-to ceiling, was in need of care. Prior to our move, my eldest son, dad and I flew out to spend several days working on the house. Even after that, it still was inadvisable for us to live in. Drastic measures needed to be taken; so, I hired help.

My neighbor, Cody, a tall, white haired, rosy cheeked, genuinely good man, very much enjoyed having "Levi the Amish guy" work on his house, so one afternoon, shortly after we settled into our home, he brought Levi over so that I could show him what needed to be done and to see if he would be right for the job. I was nervous about having Levi come to my house because I'd never talked to an Amish person before and I had all

1

these preconceived notions. Unsure how to behave, I fretted about the possibility of somehow doing or saying something that would cause offense.

Cody introduced Levi to us. Levi was a man of shorter stature and slight build. He had a long disheveled, dark brown beard, and friendly blue eyes. He was in typical Amish dress; tan straw hat, blue-gray long-sleeved button-up shirt, black suspenders, black pants and black shoes. Levi was very kind and easy to talk to; which surprised me. Our neighbor hung out visiting with my children while I talked with Levi outside. Right away he noticed the Oregon license plates on my van.

"Ohhhhhhh," he crooned. "You are from OR-re-GUN, huh?" This was said with great emphasis while slowly nodding his head. "I know about that place."

I looked at him with eyes wide, mouth gaping open enough for Missouri's abundant insects to enter and wondered how he could possibly know about "that place;" believing whatever it was he knew wasn't good.

Tilting my head to the left, a puzzled look on my face, I inquired of him, "What do you know about that place?"

He then offered a story the likes of which I never imagined I'd hear.

Levi went on. "A few years back, when I was single, I took a train trip out west with three Amish couples and another single Amish man. We stopped in several places; Montana, Colorado, Utah, Southern California, Seattle, Washington and... Portland, Oregon."

"We had a few hours to kill at the Portland train depot while waiting for our connecting train. With not much else to do, we wandered around but stayed in the station.

A particular tall, thin, slouching black man wearing dark, baggy clothing took an interest in us. He'd watch us from a distance for a while and then approach us to ask a question or tell us something. He'd leave and then come back to talk with us again. That went on for some time.

At one point our group split up; five of us went to the gift shop and Chester, the other single man, went to use the restroom. The black man followed him and waited for the right moment. After Chester completed using the facilities, the man stretched his hand out, slammed Chester against the wall, roughed him up and demanded his wallet. Stunned, Chester handed it over and just that fast, the black man was gone."

Levi concluded "Of all the places we visited, Portland left the greatest impression."

Great, I thought, that's his impression of where I was born and raised; dangerous and full of violent criminals. I assured him I wasn't like that and that's one of the reasons we left the West, for a more rural, Christian valued society. I didn't know if he believed me at first, but he did agree to come back another day to install the wood burning stove downstairs.

"If you cannot be thankful for what you have received, be thankful for what you have escaped." —*Amish Proverb*

Levi installing my woodstove

2

Misconceptions

A few weeks after our first meeting, on a cool August morning I found myself traveling down a narrow dirt road surrounded by lush green pastures and rolling hills to pick up Levi and Lester, his work companion for the day. I'd never met Lester before. He was a very tall, scrawny young man who looked and acted as though he'd just seen a ghost; "perhaps he hadn't much interaction with the non-Amish" I surmised to myself.

Upon arriving at my home, they bounded out of the van before I even came to a complete stop and quickly got to work unloading their tools from the trunk. Leading the men up the porch steps, which too, were in need of repair, I showed Levi and Lester into the house through the living room door. A large framed looking glass hung prominently on the barn red colored living room wall. Being under the impression that mirrors were forbidden in the Amish world, I was nervous about it being there and the Amish men seeing themselves in it. Foolishly, I believed that Levi and Lester had never looked in one before, thus having no idea what they looked like. To my surprise the duo didn't even notice the looking glass as I continued leading them on through the dining room, into the hallway and straight downstairs where they would be installing the woodstove.

Checking things out, Levi asked me for a small mirror so he could look into my already existing ninety-five-year-old chimney to make sure it was safe for a woodstove installation. Digging around, I found a small rectangle shaped cosmetic mirror in my purse and hesitatingly handed it to him. That worried me, again, because after all, I believed that he couldn't look at his own reflection in a mirror due to his rigid religious beliefs, and here I was, aiding him in committing a sin. Levi seemed perfectly comfortable with the object, using it as needed; all the while behaving normally. That confused me.

Within two hours the woodstove was installed, and the men were ready to return to their country homes. Tools packed up, Levi determinedly jumped into the van's front seat, while Lester, eyes down and shoulders drawn in, not wanting to draw attention to himself, dutifully sat on the bench behind us, perhaps out of respect for his elder. I wouldn't have known he was there if I hadn't watched him get into the van.

I was a very curious and determined person; if I wanted something, or wanted to know something, I would ask.

"Hey, Levi, do you mind if I pick your brain about something?" I queried. "Something about your lifestyle as an Amish man, in particular?" I continued.

Nodding his head with a slight tilt to the right, his beard moving in sync, he agreed. Whew, taking a deep breath and getting up my nerve; keeping the shakiness in my voice under wraps; and knowing I must have sounded kooky to him I inquired, "Are you allowed to look into a mirror?" A smile crept across his lips; his eyes lit up. Levi looked at me and with a chuckle, assured me, "yes, we have mirrors in our homes." Elaborating, "We have small mirrors at the wash basin to use when brushing our hair, washing our face, and putting our hats or caps on."

"Oh, now don't I feel foolish and naive," I thought to myself, hoping Levi didn't see the embarrassment written all over my face. For the duration of the trip I bravely asked him the questions that were burning in my mind. I could not ask him everything due to time constraints.

I was happy to get back home to my children after dropping them off. Like most families, we had traditions. As part of our evening as we dined together and I'd ask each of the children what was good about their day. That night's main topic of discussion was the Amish. Everyone had their turn talking, and then it was Jerry's chance. Having the Amish men in our home was his positive event for the day. Jerry, my random, witty, blue eyed, freckled faced eight-year-old boy, expressed what he thought of the Amish men, "They look like they are from New York" he quipped. At that affirmative statement from my boy, I covered my mouth stifling a giggle so as not to embarrass him. "That's interesting," I replied. "Jerry, you have never been to New York; but I suppose it's a possibility."

"Our duty is not to see through one another, but to see one another through." —*Amish Proverb*

Mirror typically found in an Amish home

3

First time in an Amish Home

After Levi and Lester completed installing our downstairs wood stove, I drove them home. Lester was dropped off first. We had previously arranged for me to go into Levi's home to see his cookstove. Sure, we had a woodstove installed downstairs now; however, we wanted one installed on the main floor of the house as well. To have that done we'd have to either build a new chimney or have triple-lined piping installed. Levi wanted to show me how the cookstove was installed in his home because it might have been an option for our second wood stove.

I headed down the highway and then turned down Levi's gravel road which was narrow and littered with potholes. The Amish had a joke, "Do you know what makes a good driver?" "One that can hit all the potholes." It was a bumpy, treacherous ride, which didn't help the nervousness welling up inside me knowing I would soon be in an Amish home for the first time.

With a left turn down a short driveway, and a circle in the roundabout I found myself parked in front of Levi's plain, two story white home. With a blank look on my face and now ashen skin, I got out of my van to follow

Levi up the steps, onto the wooden porch and through the simple white front door.

With great hesitation, I slipped into the home with just enough room to shut the door, placing myself to the left. I reminded myself of how Lester would behave, blending in. Five little children, thin and happy, dressed in plain blue and black clothing were playing, or helping their mother in the kitchen. Saloma, Levi's wife, a short woman of medium build, was in the kitchen at the large black cookstove making dinner. The house was warm in temperature and impressively neat and clean; especially for a family having five very young children. Glossy, butterscotch colored oak floors spanned the house wall-to wall. Simple neutral-colored wooden chairs, cabinets and tables furnished the living room, dining room and kitchen, accentuated by sapphire blue cushions, and area rugs. Simple sapphire blue homemade polyester curtains covered the windows, hung up by nails and string.

I stood there trying to blend in by holding up the wall. A calming, sublime feeling enveloped me as I took it all in. I had to forcefully calm my breathing and hold back my tears. It was all so simple, yet there was a very special feeling in the home; a feeling I'd never felt in a home before.

Levi introduced his wife Saloma to me, who paused from her kitchen duties just long enough to look at me and extend a timid "hi". Saloma in her simple black head scarf and soiled cornflower blue dress and tan apron looked exhausted; but her natural beauty shone through. I could sense the goodness radiating from her. I was intrigued by Saloma. I wanted to talk to her more; to get to know her.

My attention turned back to Levi as he showed me the cookstove and explained how it would work in my home. Levi allowed me to take photos of the stove so I could show my husband, and we could make our decision. After a little small talk and a promise to get back to him, I left. I wanted to stay. I was drawn to them. I knew there was something special about them. Little did I know at that time the huge part of my life the Amish would play.

"Homes are simple, uncluttered and clean; the outside reflects the inside." —*Amish Proverb*

Amish cookstove

4

Second Meeting

Two years ago, upon moving to the Midwest, I became quite interested in local Amish communities. Their lifestyles and customs intrigued me as a newcomer to the area. To my delight, I met a petite older lady from church who said that she was a friend and neighbor of the Amish. Her name was Isabel and she piqued my curiosity when she offered to introduce me to them. I seriously doubted that anyone would be able to personally interact, let alone be friends with people who were traditionally perceived as isolated.

Isabel offered to take me to the Amish stores near her community and to introduce me to the owners. A few days later on a hot, muggy August morning she picked me up in her black Chevy sedan. I felt uneasy; my stomach was churning. I knew nothing of the Amish. I had no idea how to behave around them, what to say to them, or if I should say anything at all to them.

Our first stop was at Lena's. She and her daughters ran a bakery selling homemade candies, cakes, pies and bread made fresh daily in their kitchen using their cookstove. They also sold free range chicken eggs to the public and to local stores. Isabel pulled into Lena's long narrow tree-lined driveway, which was accentuated with bright yellow goldenrod, giving it a warm, happy feel. There was a sign that simply read "Bakery, open Friday and Saturday."

Off to our left, surrounded by tall dried-up weeds, was what looked to be a metal shack made of rusty, apparently previously used, corrugated tin panels. I later found out that was the home of Lena's newlywed son and daughter-in-law.

A very large, vibrant flower garden and three half circle transparent plastic greenhouses were within sight as we neared the main house. Isabel parked the car next to a white wooden fence surrounding a two-story white house, and a pristine green lawn beautified with flowers of yellow mums, orange cosmos, and red cannas. I was led through a white wooden gate, up a concrete walk, and through the back door of the house into Lena's very large washroom.

Upon opening the painted white wooden door, I was met with the aroma of mouthwatering baked goods. To my left were shelves chock-full of deeply colorful woven throw rugs and, of course, Lena's baked goods. To my right was a shelf stuffed with handmade woven baskets of all shapes and sizes for sale. I was surprised the floor, made of concrete, had a drain in the middle. It was also used as a washroom, Amish for laundry room. Close by the drain sat an old fashioned, white enamel Maytag wringer washer, a few tin washtubs and a garden hose. I'd never been in such a room before, nor seen such a washer.

Within a few moments of walking in, Lena appeared on the landing leading to the main part of her house. She was a middle-aged woman of average height with tanned skin and dirty bare feet. Her hands were strong, and her shoulders broad. She wore a simple blue-gray soiled dress, brown apron and shabby white cap which concealed her hair. Lena's face was flushed and her face and bare forearms were beaded with perspiration from the heat of her cookstove as she'd obviously been baking to fill her stores shelves.

Upon seeing Isabel, Lena's eyes brightened and her lips turned up into a welcoming smile. She quickly descended the landing and they embraced each other, stood back smiling at one another and then chatted away like old friends. All the while I nervously stood there, observing both with my eyes and my heart. Something about Lena warmed me inside. I could tell she was a very special woman. I'd read very little about the Amish, I'd seen few references about the Amish in the media and had no experience interacting with them. To me they seemed so peculiar. Out of respect for them and fearing I would do or say something offensive to them, or embarrassing to me; I quietly stood by the door and watched. I also wondered what Lena was thinking of me, or if she even noticed me? Thus, I decided it best I not speak unless spoken to.

With their little chat over, Isabel turned her attention back to me, introducing Lena and me to each other. I let out a deep breath and relaxed for the first time since arriving. Lena put me at ease with her direct eye contact and open, honest manner. I felt relieved I could be myself around her; it was quite amazing actually.

After that I was included in the conversation. I shopped a little, choosing a fuzzy, golden-colored woven throw rug and a few dozen brown chicken eggs. Then we were on our way. I enjoyed the visit so much; I hated to leave.

Since that first meeting Lena and I have become dear friends. Our religious differences, lifestyle differences, and backgrounds don't matter because in our hearts, we were very much the same. We were just two mothers of many (between us we have seventeen children, six from me, eleven from her...gasp!) raising our families the best we could. I always greeted her or left her with a hug. There truly was something special about that charming lady. My life was richer because of her.

I was a trifle more at ease as we headed to our next stop. We drove down Lena's long driveway back to the main highway. Then we turned onto another highway that had evidence of Amish...horse apples (horse manure) in the road. Up a little further was a yellow diamond shape

"Share the Road" sign with a silhouette of a buggy on it. Finally, we turned left onto a road dotted with several white two-story Amish homes on farms littered with rusty horse drawn equipment reminiscent of the 1800's. Buggies were parked in yards with chickens running about, while cows and horses grazed in the nearby pastures. Small, barefooted children dressed in typical Amish clothing of solid and subdued colors walked along the road waving and smiling at every passing vehicle.

Up a little farther a small white homemade sign hanging between two wooden posts read "Sunny Pastures Country Store" written in black paint. We pulled in the short dirt driveway and parked next to a deck attached to a long brown building with a green metal roof that apparently was the store. Isabel led the way up the stairs and through the weather worn wooden door. Sylvia, a tall middle-aged woman with beautiful skin, soft features, and graying hair peeping out from her white cap above her dark brown eyes, sat at a desk in the corner next to a black wood stove. She was the owner of the store. Isabel introduced me to her and told Sylvia I'd just moved there from the West Coast. Isabel and Sylvia chatted and laughed like old friends. I found Sylvia to be a very lighthearted, jovial lady.

After inspecting the few shelves lined with mostly dried goods of pasta, cereal, and baking supplies, I set a few items on Sylvia's desk to purchase. She had no formal check out station like in the stores I was used to. Sylvia opened the top desk drawer, pulled out a pen and receipt book to neatly hand write down each item, quantity and price. She then bagged the items in plastic bags and totaled the tab, adding it up using her mind and pen, the old-fashioned way. I paid her cash, as that was the only option, then said goodbye.

As we drove out of the community to return home Isabel pointed out people's homes that she knew. "There is Elmer Yutzi's home; he's a chicken farmer who also has nine children. There's old John Schrock's home. He lost his wife to cancer a few years ago. That small house on the left near the road, with the dog lying on the porch, belongs to a young married couple – Jerry and Anna. Anna hails from Central Missouri, as many of the Amish in this community do.

I had no idea how I would ever remember, number one, where the stores were located and number two; everybody's name. How grateful I was that Isabel reached out to me and generously took the time to show me around to introduce me to the Amish people. Little did I know at that time what an impact they would have on my life and that of my family? As new families moved into my community, I too had the opportunity to introduce them to the Amish and the blessings that came from associating with them.

"We need old friends to help us grow old and new friends to help us stay young." —*Letty Cottin Pogrebin*

Sylvia's handwritten receipt

5

The Beginning

September 18, 2015, is a day I'll always remember. It was the day an idea was planted in my mind that forever changed the course of my life.

After having been introduced to the Amish and their stores by my friend Isabel, I'd become a regular customer. On that warm mid-September day my three young daughters; Hannah, 14, Adeline 11, and Violet 3, our neighbor, her daughter and I paid a visit to Sylvia's store. We rode in my husband's gray, beefy crew cab diesel truck instead of my twelve-passenger van, which I usually took on outings. My neighbor, Lucinda, was looking for mineral salt. Sylvia did not carry it in her store and suggested we drive half a mile down to the first house on the left, that of Eddie and Ester's.

Always up for an adventure, setting aside our uneasy feelings, we drove to Eddie and Ester's. How weird was the situation? There was a truck full of people from the city going to a complete stranger's house to inquire about purchasing salt. Never would I have dreamed of doing such a thing in the big city; one was liable to have their safety threatened in a variety of ways: by attacking dogs, guns, or having objects thrown at them. Life in the country was different though; a friendlier, more trusting place I was learning.

Eddie and Ester lived down a dirt road, lined on both sides by ditches, littered with ruts and potholes. Thankfully the black mailbox in front of their house had Eddie's name displayed on it or we might not have known we were at the right place. You see, we were expecting to see a store, something similar to Sylvia's. What we saw was a plain two story, white house attached to another plain two-story white house, several outbuildings of various sizes, mostly built of rusty scrap tin, and a very large vegetable garden; but no store.

Turning the truck left into the lane (country for driveway I learned) I had to swerve this way and that to avoid pits. I couldn't avoid the deep rut however. Giggling noises came from the bench behind me; the girls were enjoying the ride. Not sure where to park, I chose a spot next to the hitching post where horses and buggies were to be tied.

Lucinda and I looked at each other with questioning expressions, confused as to what we should do next. "Should we go knock on the door to see if someone answers, or drive away hoping nobody saw us and purchase the salt at Wal-Mart instead?" With our lack of experience in dealing with the Amish we were at a loss; we hated to intrude upon their quiet life. My middle daughter questioned me as to what I was thinking, "Should we go, or shouldn't we go, Mom?"

Before we could do anything, curiosity won Lucinda over. She boldly jumped out of the truck, raced past the hitching post, along the concrete path onto the weather worn porch and knocked on the white door that was covered with many smudges of handprints. A few moments later, a very thin, middle-aged woman of average height, with nut brown skin from many days of hard work in the sun, cautiously opened the door, just enough to peak her head out. Seeing it was only a petite gray-haired woman, Ester felt it safe to step onto the porch, bringing into full view her simple gray-blue dress, dark brown apron soiled from her cooking, and bare feet. Ester greeted Lucinda, not with a word, but with a reserved, distrusting expression. Not one to be shy, Lucinda responded with a warm greeting, introducing herself and sharing that Sylvia suggested we come by for some mineralized salt. At that, Ester's expression relaxed. Indeed, Ester had some salt for sale.

Meanwhile the rest of us sat quietly in the truck, mesmerized by what was occurring, not wanting to miss a thing. I couldn't stand it any longer. I had to get out to hear what was going on, so I joined Lucinda on the porch. Ester was happy to inform us that she also sold garden produce and raw milk. Lucinda and I purchased salt from her, and after that I became a regular milk customer as well.

It was a quick visit, as Ester was a woman of few words, even though Lucinda could carry on a conversation for hours single handedly.

We returned to the truck, seated ourselves, buckled up and were ready to head out when a beanstalk of a man, who appeared to be in his forties, with a weathered face, and a curly gray beard tickling the collar of his homemade gray/blue shirt, flagged us down. Here again was a situation in which Lucinda and I weren't sure how to behave. "Should I stop? Was he mistaking us for someone else? Was I seeing things?" I wondered. We stopped.

Making a circular motion with his scrawny right arm, knobby fingers formed into a fist, he motioned Lucinda to roll her window down. She did. He then walked right up to the truck, folded his arms across his chest and rested them in the window opening, leaning in close to Lucinda. "His behavior was quite overt for an Amish man," I thought.

"Hello, my name is Eddie," he greeted us in a high-pitched voice. Raising one eyebrow, nodding his head slowly, he continued in his uniquely Eddie accent, coupled with his natural Pennsylvania Deutsch accent. "What a nice truck you have....eh," adding emphasis with a broad, partially toothless grin.

Eyes darting around, obviously inspecting the inside of the truck, he proceeded "And this truck seats six... and it has four doors and is diesel?" All the while he slowly nodded, with a delighted expression. "Is this truck yours?" he asked Lucinda who was sitting in the front passenger seat. "The truck is mine" I eagerly piped up, wondering where Eddie was going with that.

Eyes wide, smile even larger, and bouncing a little, he asked, "Would you be open to driving for the Amish?"

"Sure, I'll consider it." I blurted out, without thinking. He then continued with a big grin and twinkling eyes, "We pay very good; $0.75 cents per mile."

"Do you have a pen and paper...eh?" he asked me. Digging through my purse, I found a pen and paper for him. Using the truck hood as a desk, in very neat cursive, he wrote his and his wife's first and last names along with his address, and then enthusiastically returned the paper and pen back to me. "May I have your name and phone number?" I dutifully, as legibly as possible, wrote that down and gave it to him. "Thank you" he said, waving the paper in the air. With another smile, he was off back to his chores. For a moment, there we remained...perplexed at what had just happened.

I came to, still in a daze, and managed to get us home safely. The conversation on the trip home was filled with speculation, chatter and laughter. My daughter Hannah piped up from the back, in her matter-of-fact tone, "Well, that was weird." None of us was sure what to make of the situation. I wondered "What just happened there? Would anyone believe it?" And "Where did we move our family to? The Twilight Zone?"

That evening, I re-read what Eddie wrote down. He didn't leave a phone number and yet he asked for mine. I found that puzzling. I later learned that he had access to a phone in a shack located on a non-Amish person's property. That phone was only good for making calls out; it could not receive calls.

What an unusual day that had been. Little did I know that the impromptu meeting with Eddie would be the beginning of a new life for me. Eddie was a unique character; we will always remember him.

"Opportunity may knock once, but temptation bangs on your front door forever." —*Amish Proverb*

Sign typically seen in or near an Amish community

6

Becoming Official

After my introduction to Eddie, I called a fellow church member, Keith Brady, an elderly man, and jack of all trades. He

had been "hauling" the Amish the past fifteen years. Relaying to him the encounter with Eddie and my desire to haul a little bit using my twelve-passenger van, Keith suggested I get started by making a flyer to put up in the Amish stores. With his guidance I came up with my fees charging $0.80 cents per mile loaded and $0.40 cents per mile empty and a $20 a night layover fee after two nights being away.

In addition, as a man who has worked alongside them in construction, as well as for them as a driver, Keith kindly offered his wisdom in how to deal with the Amish. He offered, "They are good people. Once they get to know and trust you, they'll do anything for you."

Then he cautioned, "They like to get the best deal and may try to talk you down or gripe and complain. Some of them will trash your van and even vandalize it. So, you have to watch."

Continuing, "Some of them like to cram as many passengers into the van as possible so they can save a few dollars. It is your choice. You can allow that to happen, or not."

"Okay..." I muttered, taking it all in.

"As far as their children go, generally they don't like to sit in car seats because they are used to moving around in the buggy and their parents don't make them. Mothers like to hold their infants in their laps. You have to decide your policy on that as well."

"Uh huh," I responded

"They are hardworking people and can smell bad at times." He persisted, "They will call you all hours of the day and night; sometimes they will want to go on a long trip at the very last minute."

Proceeding, Keith emphasized, "Always be on time, be honest and be dependable and you'll always have business."

He left me with one final thought, "It's not an easy job to be a driver, but it is rewarding."

It was a lot to absorb. I was grateful for his time and wisdom as it prepared me for my first call.

"No dream comes true until you wake up and go to work."
—*Amish Proverb*

My 15-passenger van used to haul Amish

7

First call to Haul

Putting the final touches on our Christmas décor; dusting shelves, mopping floors, baking cookies, and wrapping gifts to the joyous melodies of Christmas carols; the bustle of preparing for the Christmas holiday was in full force. This was our first Christmas in our new home and it was going to be just the eight of us; something I was very happy about.

Amidst the preparations, my phone belted out "Angels we have heard on high, sweetly singing o'er the plains." A phone number I didn't recognize popped up on the caller ID. Suspiciously, believing the caller to be a telemarketer, I answered the phone with a reserved "Hello."

"Is this Haley?" abruptly questioned the deep, fast-paced voice on the other end of the line. Not sure if I wanted to admit it was indeed Haley, I sighed, responding with a weak "Yes."

"This is David B from Mt. Vernon, Missouri. Can you drive a group of us to Marion, Kentucky for Christmas leaving tomorrow at noon?" he

blurted out as I made my way up the narrow stairwell to my bedroom so I could have quiet from the children.

"Yes," I affirmed, "I could do that." Now I was visibly shaking. I couldn't believe what I'd just committed myself to; and at Christmas, without first discussing it with my husband.

"What do you run per mile?" David demanded.

"I run at $0.80 cents," I told him.

"That is way too high; we won't pay it. There are only eight people going down," he grumbled. "I will see if I can get a different driver with a smaller van so it will be cheaper."

"Okay." I murmured, confused by his curtness with me.

Before I let him hang up (because deep down, I had a feeling he wouldn't find anyone else) I asked him, since there would be plenty of seats available in the van, and with-it being Christmas, if I could bring my three youngest children. He responded with a quick, and seemingly annoyed, "Yes."

"I will call you tomorrow morning by 7:30 a.m. if I can't find another driver," he pronounced, followed by a firm "Goodbye."

At that, I wondered to myself if our brief exchange was the extent of Amish social skills in dealing with outsiders.

That was it; that was our conversation. I was all nerves. I'd never been called to haul before and that was very last minute, giving me little time to prepare mentally and physically, plus that man appeared to be quite rude. In addition, the idea of driving to Kentucky filled me with apprehension. Never had I driven so far; thirteen hours on my own in one day; which is how long the trip would take. Should I tire, there was no other driver that could cover me, the Amish don't drive. The most I'd driven in one shot was six hours straight. I'd be on my own for that one; going to a place I'd never been with people I'd never met in addition to having so little rest on that first night to prepare myself for such a demanding task.

Still on edge, I slumped downstairs and confessed to my husband what I'd committed myself to and asked the three youngest if they'd like to join me, which they did.

Restlessly, I fussed around the house planning what to bring if I were to get a call back in the morning booking the trip. Being so fuzzy brained, snacks were all I managed to figure out.

Decorations done, house as clean as it was going to get, and gifts wrapped, it was time for bed. The children gathered around me while I read them Christmas stories, then tucked them in. Full of nervous energy I puttered around and then finally went to bed after 1:00 a.m., though I hardly slept. I wanted so badly to go to Kentucky for Christmas with the Amish, yet felt torn about our family being apart during the holiday.

"Don't fear tomorrow or regret the past. Live for what's now and never look back." —*Satchel Paige*

Amish phone shack

8

First Day of Hauling

The next morning...

While tossing and turning beneath my thick winter bedclothes the Christmas Carol, "Angels we have heard on high, sweetly singing o'er the plain" jolted me awake. I knew David B was on the other end of the line and I knew what he was going to tell me. He agreed to pay my price of $0.80 cents per mile and the trip was a go. I was to pick him up at noon at the furniture shop on State Highway 96. I had no idea where that was, which only added fuel to my already frazzled nerves.

Adrenaline rushing through my veins I was wide awake. As quickly and as quietly as possible, so the children could continue sleeping, I packed my bags, the children's bags and toys, and gifts for the children to open on Christmas day. I did a quick check on the van and was, at least physically, ready to go.

Before my three youngest children, Jerry age 9, Jack age 6, and Violet, age 3, and I embarked on our first trip with the Amish, my husband and older three children met us in the living room to pray. Humbly kneeling in a circle on the hard wood floors, Christmas lights shimmering in the background, my husband offered a sincere prayer of thanksgiving for our abundant blessings and petitioned the Lord for our safety while apart.

We hugged each other and were off on our new adventure. The children were excited. Me? I was too, but for the time being I was more apprehensive, wondering what I'd gotten myself into. I popped a Christmas carol CD into the player and focused on the joyous music, hoping it would help me relax as we traveled the twenty miles to David B's furniture shop.

I pulled into the gravel lane of the furniture shop, which was in fact a large metal building. Standing on the concrete landing next to the shop's side door, waiting for me, was David B. He was a tall, broad-shouldered man, and wide of girth. He had a commanding appearance. From our conversation on the phone, he looked nothing like I expected.

Neatly dressed in a black felt hat, black vest, homemade sapphire blue long sleeve shirt, black trousers and black shoes, his piercing green eyes met mine as I pulled the van next to him, re-kindling the apprehension I felt before. Passing in front of me, he opened the passenger door, and without any conversation, hopped in and started giving me orders.

He told me to drive further up the lane to his house and pick up his family. My three children, with their mouths agape became very still on the bench behind me. The four of us watched in awe as this family of strangers, David's wife Alma and three of his ten children loaded their belongings and themselves into our van. None of them said a word to us. Next David commanded me to drive to his friends Ezra and Becky's home down the highway a short distance. Pulling down their wide gravel lane, an elderly couple, silver-haired, and bent with age, upon hearing the van, exited the small white home to our right, while a few others exited the larger two-story home on our left.

David jumped out of the van, greeted everyone and conversed in Pennsylvania Deutsch. The children and I sat quietly watching and listening with great interest. The van's two side doors were opened, exposing my three children on the front bench, as the Amish started filing into the middle seat. My passengers greeted me with scowls. One man in particular, thin, small framed, and in his late 30's was very upset with me; speaking to me in a chastising tone, "Why are all these children here? We have old people traveling; they need more room?"

I noticed another man, elderly, with a rugged nose and pale skin. He made a particularly nasty face at me then turned away from the van. The younger man and the older man returned after some discussion. The younger one, again berating me, spat, "You know; it is Christmas?

This man wants to go see his family." I sat there thinking, "I'd like to be with my family on Christmas, too; and I'm leaving half of them home to take these people to see their family."

David had given me permission to bring the children. Why had I agreed to do this? Why was he treating me this way? The younger man returned, irritated, and said to me, "When he saw how many children you had with you, he decided not to go on the trip. It would be too crowded. I had to convince him to go anyway." Getting agitated, I finally told him, "Yes, it is Christmas, and I wanted my children with me. There is enough room for everyone." Hoping to soften things, "I understand this was a last-minute trip and am glad he decided to go."

With everyone loaded up, offering a silent, sincere prayer of comfort for me, safety on the trip, and that my children would behave, we were off on our first trip with the Amish. What a way to start a trip. I hoped the next few days would be better than what we'd experienced so far.

"It is better to give others a piece of your heart than a piece of your mind." —*Amish Proverb*

Amish home

9

A Christmas unlike any other

I was still wide awake at 2:00 a.m., when we pulled into Elmer's, David's brother-in-law's, gravel lane. From the dim twinkling of the stars, I could barely make out the two story, white house on our left, and brown metal, one story shop in front of us. There I was directed to park the van. Opening my door so I could step out and stretch, I heard the cooing, screeching and chattering of the country's wildlife. Then the stench of hogs drifted into my nostrils causing me to nearly retch.

A flashlight shone from within the house, and out came Elmer, a short, dark-haired man with a round nose. He helped David's family settle into the home. I sat in my van, with the door closed, watching and wondering what would happen next. About ten minutes later David and Elmer returned to the van to ask me what I wanted to do. They suggested I might want to stay the remainder of the night in the shop. It was a wide-open space with plenty of room for the boys to run around. There was a cookstove in it, as well as mattresses to sleep on. It would be plenty comfortable for us he assured me. I agreed to stay in the shop and then decide what to do the next day.

The shop had a concrete floor and building materials stood along the wall edges. There were several windows and two back rooms. It was cold and dark making it the perfect spot to catch a few hours of much needed rest. We shivered ourselves to blissful sleep under blankets and thick quilts provided by our Amish hosts.

After a few hours of sleep we awoke, cold and hungry. The children were excited. I hadn't decided how I felt. Someone politely knocked on the shop door. Not sure what that was about, I called "come in." A young barefoot girl wearing a dainty white cap, simple blue dress and brown apron, entered the room carrying a large gray metal tray. She walked across the concrete floor to the folding table near our beds and set the tray down. It was our breakfast; fresh milk, two different kinds of boxed cereals and sugar, along with spoons and stainless-steel bowls to eat with. That was much unexpected.

With breakfast completed, the children and I changed out of the clothes we had slept and traveled in. We were wondering what to do with the day, when we heard another knock on the door. Again, I invited them in. This time it was a boy about twelve. He wore no hat exposing his bowl cut hair and wore his work clothing; a stained cotton shirt, leather suspenders, and patched up trousers. Behind him, he pulled a little red wagon loaded with chopped wood. He started a fire in the cookstove for us, then, without saying a word, eft.

We hung out in the shop for a while. The children stayed occupied by opening the gifts I had brought for them and playing with their toys.

Our next visitor was David B. He came to ask if we would be staying in the shop or going to a hotel. I decided we'd rather stay with the Amish, even if it was in the shop. It certainly was an experience. David was happy with that decision because, as he plainly stated, "it would save us a lot of money."

Reality was setting in. It was Christmas and we were in Kentucky, with strangers, away from the rest of our family. Still not sure how to behave, or what the boundaries were as far as staying on Amish property,

I thought it best to keep to ourselves that Christmas day. After playing a few games with the children's new toys, we tired of hanging out in the shop.

I opened the door and decided to look around the property. We walked to the back field and watched the sheep grazing on corn stubble in their woolly winter coats. The malodorous, obese, ornery pigs caught our attention as they were wallowing noisily in a mud hole behind a hand-made wooden fence. A variety of different breeds of chickens wandered about pecking at gravel and hunting for seeds.

Violet, my youngest, gleefully chased the chickens around hoping to catch one. At the cackling of the chickens and the laughing of my children, we felt someone watching us from the house. I was so glad to have that time to focus on my three youngest children without all the 'I have to do's' at home that distracted me from spending quality time with them. What a blessing our time together was.

We went back to the shop and shortly thereafter a fourth knock resounded on the door. That time, it was Orpha, Elmer's tall, brown eyed, rosy cheeked wife coming to show me how to keep the fire going in the cookstove.

Afternoon came and the children were hungry again. We had a lunch made of supplies I had brought along, peanut butter and jelly sandwiches, carrot sticks and cookies, like an impromptu picnic at the folding table in the shop.

The very out of the ordinary Christmas day went on and on; I was desperately hoping we'd be invited for Christmas supper. My backup plan was to find a Denny's Restaurant or Sheri's Café and Pies in the nearest big town. For years my grandfather and his wife ate their holiday meals at restaurants such as those. I reasoned, maybe it could be a new tradition for us? If nothing else, it would be a new experience.

There was pounding on the door. I opened it and there stood David B, again, cleanly shaved, eyes bright, with just a hint of a smile gracing his face. He asked if we'd like to join the family for Christmas supper.

Controlling my elation; I REALLY wanted to jump up and down and scream with joy; I calmly responded, "Yes. We'd love to. Thank you, David." David then told us when to be ready and asked if I would drive everyone to the home where supper would be served. "Happily!" I agreed.

"Loving does not empty the heart, nor giving empty the purse."
—*Amish Proverb*

Shop we stayed in

10

Feeling Famous

With a skip in my step, I anticipated our first Christmas Supper with the Amish. I grabbed a baby wipe to wash the dirt off the children's faces, arms and hands so they would be presentable to go to Christmas Supper. They didn't have to wear fancy clothing, but it had to be clean, which they balked at. Each child chose a toy or two to bring to the home we would dine at. I chose a toy as well, my crocheting. Then we were as ready as we would ever be.

Meeting David and his family at the van, we drove about a mile down the road. Then David instructed me to pull off down a narrow gravel lane which ended in a circle drive. Bustling with activity, children of all ages and sizes, in their freshly washed and impeccably ironed Sunday best clothing, were running about. The small porch and surrounding yard were crowded with dozens of men in black slacks, crisp white shirts, and black felt hats who were visiting, and smoking. I hadn't realized that the Amish smoked.

Assortments of black buggies were pulling in; their horses were unhitched and put in the barn so they could share in their

Christmas supper. Several minivans and fifteen passenger vans dropped off Christmas guests as well. It appeared as though the small gray, two story saltbox style home did not have enough room to contain all the arriving visitors.

I parked our van alongside the buggies. Arms loaded with toys, the four of us guardedly walked up on to the crowded porch, past groups of men, through the metal door, and into the house. Characteristic of most Amish homes the living room, dining room and kitchen were sort of a communal room with just a door which opened up to stairs leading to the top floor. The living room was crowded with various shapes and sizes of Amish men in their Sunday best. Some were sitting at folded tables, playing board games, while others stood chatting amongst themselves.

The women in their freshly pressed white Sunday prayer Kapp's *, dresses held together with straight pins and neatly pleated white aprons bustled about the kitchen making the final preparations for the Christmas supper. The children, ranging from infants to teens, congregated between both rooms, playing on the floor or among the three rows of highly polished wooden benches which were set up for additional seating. Violet, Jerry, Jack and I weren't sure where to go, so we decided it best to settle ourselves in the middle row of the benches and visit with the Amish children.

Settled in, I was hoping we would blend in. Of course, it didn't work. Nobody talked to us, but, boy, did they stare; the children especially. Oblivious to their surroundings, my sons pulled out their Christmas toys; a Hot Wheels dragon track that shot fire and fancy, vibrantly colored Hot Wheel cars. Violet unpacked the doll, pretend food and dishes, and books from her pink teddy bear backpack. The Amish children had toys as well. The little boys had a 1980's Little People garage, a few little people, old plastic toy cars, and a handful of plastic farm animal figures. The girls played with their homemade white faceless dolls and Amish doll clothing.

The Amish boys upon discovering my son's colorful new toys dropped their simple*r* toys and made a beeline. They had likely never seen toys such as those and they were enthralled.

Noticing their outstretched hands, my boys stopped their play to share with their new friends. From then on Amish and 'English,' or as the Amish say, Englischer, children played well together except for the few boys, who pulled and tugged at each other to get closer to my sons and their toys.

While that was going on Violet and I were having our own unique experiences. I wore a large bronze articulated owl with big shiny black eyes hanging at the end of a long necklace chain. Not long after I sat down, a little girl of about age eight planted herself on the bench, not three inches from me. She had silky chestnut hair peeking under her crisp white cap, and big green eyes. She spoke not a word to me, but reached out with her little pointer finger and poked my necklace causing the owl to dance as it hung from my neck. She poked it again, and again, and again continuing this game for quite some time. She paused only to look at my face with intense curiosity. I sat still and silent, watching her watch me with similar interest. Finally, the little girl got up and left.

She was soon replaced by a tow-headed blue-eyed boy of perhaps six years. He plopped himself practically on my lap and tilted his head up for a good view of my face. Without a word, eyes wide, he just stared at me...openly and intensely for five minutes, perhaps longer. And there I sat, focusing on my crocheting, my finger gripping the crochet string tightly. I felt uncomfortable, again. With my feet planted solidly under the bench, I pretended not to be bothered by this young boy's simple curiosity. As he scrutinized my face, apparently to find some sense of common ground, I would occasionally turn to my little bench mate and smile to acknowledge his presence. It was hard enough feeling comfortable in an Amish home at Christmas, without the admiring, unrelenting gaze of my curious little friends. I certainly wasn't used to all that attention.

Violet, my sweet three-year-old, got the most attention. Her gorgeous thick blonde hair cascaded midway down her back forming ringlets. Her large, exquisite clear blue eyes and her porcelain cheeks kissed with freckles caused much of a stir among the little Amish girls. Her clothing did as well. She wore a mid-thigh length, long sleeve gray ruffled shirt and purple leggings. Several little girls, hair braided on top of their heads and wearing simple dresses, pinafores and caps took notice of Violet. Surrounding her, eyes wide with wonder, they stared at her. Little arms reached out to touch her hair. Small, delicate, curious hands rubbed the ruffles on her shirt.

Violet patiently sat on the bench allowing them to touch her, watching them just as they were watching her. Not one child said a word. After a little while, Violet, tiring of it, turned to me whispering, "They are touching me; they are touching me." Soon, little girls began pushing each other off the bench so they could sit by her, one girl on each side, and just stare at her and touch her. I couldn't believe it. I'd never seen anything like it. I wondered if they'd ever been around a little 'English' girl.'

A very petite, and sweet, articulate young girl of 8, Betty broke away from the crowd of girls surrounding Violet to talk to me. She was obviously the one the younger girls looked to, and was very curious about me and my children. I asked her a few questions about her family, and her interests. She shared that she was one of ten children, including two sets of twins. She pointed out other children in the room and told me a little about them. The children were endless. She also asked me about my family. Did I have a husband? How many children did I have? Where did I live? I was so glad to have someone to talk to. It was nice to find a friend in her for that one day, Christmas, when I was away from the rest of my own family and culture.

Adults did not speak to me except to inform me when it was time to get my children and I fed. When I asked anyone a respectful question such as "Where is the bathroom?" or "Is it okay if your children play with my children's toys?" I was given a simple, proper answer, no more, no less. From where I was sitting, I could see into the kitchen/dining room and noticed a few women glancing my way. I would have loved to talk to one of the young mothers who were sitting on a chair along the kitchen wall tending to their babies and toddlers, but I sensed a slight, invisible division of place and culture.

After about two hours, it was time to eat. The men and teenage boys filed into the living room, settling themselves into the couches, rocking chairs, and around the folding tables. The women and babies, most of them already in the dining room and kitchen common, found a seat and the children surrounded us on the benches. Finally, a woman spoke to me matter of factly and let me know that it was time to get ready for supper. So, I had my children put away their toys and sit on a bench among the other children.

That was my first time having a meal in an Amish home. I was paying close attention to everything because no one told me how things would work. With everyone seated, it got quiet. I watched as heads bowed. The children and I followed suit. We expected to hear a man offer a prayer, but that wasn't the Amish way. We heard nothing. There was, perhaps, the cooing of a baby or shuffling of a foot, but no one said anything. About two minutes later people began stirring and the teenage boys and men filed into the dining room to get their food while the women and children sat patiently and waited.

After the men loaded their plates, a woman walked over to us, inviting my children and me to fill our plates. My boys acted as if they were in heaven. Forgetting the rest of the food, they went straight for the ice cream. With seven gallons and varieties to choose from, they loaded up their plates. That's all they ate for their Christmas supper which left them hungry later that evening. Violet and I had a hard time deciding what to eat as the long dining room table was weighed down with so much food. Not one single spot was uncovered.

In addition to the ice cream for dessert, there were several varieties of homemade pies, including pecan, cherry and banana cream. There was a

Jell-O salad, pizza pasta, a large round tray of various meat and cheese slices, homemade bread, homemade butter and a variety of homemade jam. In addition, there were several dishes I didn't recognize. An orange five-gallon Tupperware water dispenser and clear disposable cups were positioned on the end of the table to wash our meal down with. I was expecting the traditional American holiday meal of turkey, stuffing, rolls, green bean casserole and cranberry sauce or something akin to it. I felt as a foreigner in this simpler yet warm and inviting environment.

The women and children got in line behind Violet and me. With plates loaded up, they went back to the kitchen to eat and visit amongst themselves. By then the men were coming back for second helpings. People began shuffling around. Those who were still eating set their utensils down. The talking ceased and as if by mutual accord, silence once more filled the house. Heads bowed and everyone offered a mute prayer of thanksgiving in their heart, marking the end of the bountiful Christmas supper.

"How we spend Christmas is of greater significance than how much we spend for it." —*Amish Proverb*

* Prayer covering or kapp, per The Apostle Paul's counsel to women in 1 Corinthians 11:5 "But every woman that prayeth or prophesieth with her head uncovered dishonoureth her head... The kapp serves as a reminder to pray continually.

Girls in their Sunday best clothing

11

Home Again

Rap tap tap, rap tap tap, rap tap tap! "Hey, Haley, are you awake?" David B's baritone voice startled me out of my deep sleep. It was only 6:00 am. "Seriously, I thought, it's time to get up already? Don't these Amish allow their drivers to get any sleep? Apparently not," I grumbled to myself.

At that I jumped out of bed quietly so as to let the children sleep a little longer. I fumbled around in the dark to my suitcase. Gathering my day clothes, dressed and quietly ventured into the cold, dark morning to load the van with our belongings that we'd packed the night before. Next, I lovingly gathered each of my sleeping children, one by one into my arms and carried them to the van.

Finally, I returned to the shop to gather our luggage and make sure we'd left it clean. Another driver had shared with me that he always left a note of thanks after staying in an Amish home, so I wrote a note and left a small gift on the folding table in the shop.

The children were still asleep as we left; I was too, though I pretended to be awake. David and his family loaded, we pick up Ezra and Becky at their son Billie's home. There waiting in front of their white two-story house with a black composition tile roof was Ezra and Becky along with their son Billie, his wife Rosanna, and their eleven children, ranging in age from late teens to an infant.

Curious, I watched as Ezra and Becky said their goodbyes to Billie's large family. The children were darling in their simple solid color home-made clothing, black bonnets, hats and suspenders. They were running all over except for two of them, the one in Billie's arms and the one in Rosanna's arms. Ezra and Becky would not be seeing Billie, Rosanna and their family for a long time, so I expected them to lovingly embrace one another as they bid farewell.

I learned the Amish were different. The children and their parents stood in a single line facing the van while Ezra and Becky walked down the row as would be done for a wedding line, saying "bye" and bending over, or reaching up to shake each one of their hands. That was very foreign to me. I've since learned that, as a general rule, the Amish refrain from public displays of affection, according to their cultural and religious practices.

By the time Ezra and Becky were loaded, about 7:00 a.m., the sun was nearly raised. Driving along, my heart filled with gratitude for the beauty of the rolling hills dotted with stones jetting from the soil, lush green meadows, and massive old oak trees. As we headed west clouds moved in, the sky darkened, and it began to rain. Claps of thunder and lightning lit up the sky. The further west we traveled, the heavier the rain came down, and the harder the wind blew. The van swayed to and fro. By the time we were a hundred miles into the trip creeks and rivers crested, fields and forests were flooded. There was water within two feet of the interstate and it was rising.

"Now Haley, this is pretty rough driving, isn't it? Driving in the wind and the rain?" David, my companion up front, teased me.

With a quick glare I retorted, "No David, I'm from Oregon, I can drive in this."

"Perhaps you can, but the tires on this van look pretty worn, you'd better take it easy." David cautioned.

"The tires on the van are fine, David." Curtly I assured him. Perhaps David was a little nervous having never ridden with me.

Driving west through Illinois the temperatures dropped, turning rain into sleet, then large snowflakes, forming a blizzard. The road became a sheet of ice and my windshield fogged up, ice formed, and combined with snow my visibility dropped to almost nothing. Fear settled into the pit of my stomach for our safety.

David, who was watching me drive, noticed my arms tense up, my grip on the steering wheel tighten, and my facial expression turn serious. I let my foot off the gas to slow down. Cautiously, I merged to move to the slow lane while semi-trucks, pickup trucks, SUV's and even cars passed me on the left.

Accusingly, David, again, questioned me, "You don't know how to drive in the snow do you?" His questioning wasn't very helpful.

"No, I don't have much experience driving in the snow. Where I come from if we get more than one half inch of snow the whole city shuts down, schools close, government offices close and most everyone stays home." I honestly replied. My truthful response did not put him at ease. I felt uneasy myself. My mind was very focused on driving as many thoughts raced through. Once again, I wondered why I had agreed to driving them.

Continuing on I heard a slow, deep, elderly male voice from the back of the van, "one, two, three, four, five, six..."

"Ezra," I hollered back to him, "what are you counting?"

"I'm counting the cars, trucks, and semis in the ditches. So far, I've counted thirty-six cars, twelve trucks, and three semis."

"Thank you, Ezra," I said thinking to myself, 'I'm not the only fool out here, and we are still on the road. So, I'm doing okay.'

Upon returning to Mt. Vernon, it was still snowing heavily, accumulating to six inches. It took us five additional hours to get home.

We were all exhausted physically and mentally, especially me. I still had miles to go beyond Mt. Vernon on hilly, winding, and curvy two-lane ice-covered snow packed roads. "Inhale, exhale, relax, inhale, exhale, relax," I told myself as we continued on.

Slowly, I took each curve, eyes darting around watching for traffic and wildlife. The roads had not been plowed, at least, not recently. As I turned on to State Highway 96, even though the highway was bad, I felt some relief knowing we were almost there. As we neared Ezra and Becky's home, Becky turned to me and sweetly offered for us to spend the night so we would be warm and safe until the roads were plowed. What a generous offer. I politely declined, anxious to return to my home and family.

After dropping off a grateful Ezra and Becky I continued to David B's home. Upon seeing David's snow-covered drive, I wondered if I'd make it out. A resurging wave of anxiety swallowed whatever resolve I had left. I hesitated as I approached.

David, in a commanding, matter of fact voice, ordered me to turn into the drive. I believed I'd get stuck; however, he seemed to think otherwise. After several failed attempts at getting the van no farther than seven feet in, David decided one of his boys would get out and fetch a sleigh to transport their belongings to their home, which was still about an eighth of a mile down the hill.

Alma, noticing my distress, very sweetly suggested to me, "I could make up beds for you and the children so you can get a good night's sleep before returning home. Perhaps by tomorrow the roads will be cleared." I didn't respond to Alma's kindness, believing David would not approve, though I would have taken her up on the offer. I was correct. David piped up, "No, she doesn't need to stay. She can make it home just fine." He looked at me with his most, yet forced, reassuring expression and Alma dropped the matter.

Passengers safely at home, I turned up the van's heat, turned on some classical music, said a silent prayer for safe travels and cautiously drove my tired self and children back to our home. We had completed our first trip with the Amish.

The next day I read on the internet about a terrible storm in the Midwest called Goliath. There was flooding, hail which, thankfully, we didn't experience, ice, snow, and wind. That was the storm we drove through. I was comforted in knowing I had made the right decisions in my driving. My passengers must have been simultaneously praying for safety. I knew   l on my shoulder all along.

"Every miracle Jesus does starts with a problem."
—*Amish Proverb*

Going into a gas station

12

Visit to the Dentist

Feeling under the weather, I was still in bed at 10:30 a.m. when my cell phone rang. It was a call from Missouri and the number wasn't in my contacts, so I suspected it was a call from the Amish. Clearing my throat, I forced myself to sound more awake than I really was as I answered the phone. The man on the other end was speaking English with a Deutsch accent so it sounded like gibberish to me. Struggling to understand, I deciphered the words Leroy who I didn't know, six people, Dalton, Dentist, and 5:00 p.m. that evening. Repeating what I thought he said, and having it confirmed, I gave Leroy an affirmative. Due to his mannerism of speech, I gathered there was some kind of dental emergency.

That trip was something I looked forward to because I'd heard about the "Amish" dentist and was very curious to see him. My six passengers and I arrived at the dentist office at about 6:15 that evening. Arriving in the village of Dalton, I was directed to park the van in front of a very modest, small, wooden two-story building which was unpainted. On the front, prominently displayed to the left of the door, was a white shingle (i.e. a white sign), that much to my surprise read Daniel Miller, Jr. D.D.S in bold black letters. That Amish dentist was indeed a real dentist. The state of the building caused me to wonder what kind of dentist ran that office. *Not a dentist I would ever visit,* I thought to myself.

Entering the building, we immediately found ourselves to be both in the waiting room, and the exam room. Upon the wall was a certificate from The American Academy of Oral Medicine bearing Daniel's name. That confused me; I didn't think the Amish went to college. My group of Amish sat themselves in padded chrome chairs lining the wall. Another patient, with gauze in her mouth, sat among them. Obviously, she'd seen the dentist; and it didn't look like it was a pleasant visit.

A young man wearing a red, plaid button up shirt and jeans, stood behind the counter. He greeted me and invited me to sign in. I looked at him and politely responded, "I am keeping all of my teeth tonight, thank you." Snickers came from my Amish passengers as they waited to have their teeth pulled.

Straight back from the waiting area, divided only by three-foot-tall swinging saloon style doors, was the operating room. There, was the dentist who appeared to be Amish with his long gray beard and dark hat. He had on a face mask and white lab coat. Tools of his trade were in hand as he was hunched over his patient. Two female assistants, in their solid color dresses, aprons, and white caps looked on. Anyone standing could see Dr. Miller and his assistants. They stopped what they were doing, looked up, smiled and said "hello" to me. I smiled back and boldly asked them if I could watch the procedure. A firm "no" came from the young man at reception desk. Disheartened, I sat down to wait for everyone else to have their teeth extracted. While making small talk with Leroy and his middle age daughter Nancy, I asked if the dentist was Amish. Leroy replied, "No, he is German Baptist*, as are his assistants."

Surprised to see a non-Amish man walk in, get forms to fill out from the reception desk, and sit down, I turned to Leroy, with more questions. He explained more to me about that particular dentist.

"Does Dr. Miller take non-Amish patients?" I wanted to know. "Yes, they take non-Amish patients." He replied.

"Do they only pull teeth here, or do they do any other dental work?" I asked.

"They only pull teeth here." Leroy responded, confirming my suspicions.

"Yikes," I thought to myself.

Leroy continued, "Fees are $40.00 per tooth extraction. When patients arrive and sign in, they pay $65.00 up front for each tooth being pulled in case the tooth extraction is more complicated."

Leroy, for example, had to have his gums cut in order to get the tooth out. He then was given stitches. His bill was $65.00 for that extraction. A refund of $25.00 would have been given upon check out if the extraction was simple.

Dr. Miller worked quickly extracting my six passengers' teeth making it a surprisingly quick visit to the dentist. The Amish folk were ready to go straight home instead of their usual running around. Perhaps the van full of suffering, drugged, bleeding, gauzed mouthed folk were feeling too miserable to enjoy going anywhere else that early evening. It was hard for them to talk, and much to my relief, it was a quiet ride home.

Breaking the silence of most of our trip home, I heard, "Watch out for that cow." Leroy's pained voice warned me as we neared his farm. There was a cow crossing the gravel road ahead. Cow disaster averted and my passengers safely home, I was unsure if I'd get home safely. Once the Amish were out of the van the "reduced engine power light" came on. The van seemed to run fine. Along the way I hit a couple of large jolting bumps going at freeway speed. Perhaps a wire was knocked loose. Whatever it was, everything worked out. How grateful I was for a new experience that day, and even more grateful to have kept all of my teeth.

"Laugh and the world laughs with you; snore and you sleep alone."
—*Anthony Burgess*

　　*The Old German Baptist Brethren (OGBB) is a break off of the German Baptist Church, formed in 1881 due to a dispute among the brethren. OGBB share similar beliefs with their Amish and Mennonite brothers and sisters in Christ, in that they reject the idea of baptizing infants. They are part of the post-reformation Anabaptists group.

Portions of this text adapted from Wikipedia's article on the Old German Baptist Brethren, used under the Creative Commons Attribution-ShareAlike License.

Dental office, has since gone out of business

13

Acceptance

After my Amish hauling business started picking up, a sweet deal of a large quantity of chocolate chips was made known to me. I requested two twenty-five-pound boxes from Levi J, whom I'd previously hired to work on my home. He was the "middle man" for that transaction. The chocolate chips came from Wisconsin and someone in his community was taking a trip up there to visit family. They would purchase the chocolate chips from their contact then deliver them to Levi, who then would sell them to me.

For some reason beyond my comprehension the bulk of the Mt. Vernon Community, many members of whom I did not yet know, got wind of my chocolate chip purchase. There was nothing unusual about it as I'd been known to purchase a hundred and fifty pounds of chocolate chips at a time. Because of my chocolate chip purchase, I became known as the "Chocolate Chip Lady" within their community.

They couldn't remember my real name, but they could remember my purchasing fifty pounds of chocolate chips, which, apparently, they found quite humorous.

Keith, the driver that mentored me in the beginning of my Amish hauling business, chuckled as he informed me of this. From that point on, when taking trips with the Amish and chocolate chip cookies were served, I would hear giggling, whispering in Pennsylvania Deutsch and see covert glances in my direction. I always knew what they were joking about. Keith informed me that the giving of nicknames by the Amish to the English means you've been accepted. How glad I was to be accepted.

Chocolate Chip Cookies

From Kingston Wisconsin Community Favorites - Lavern Mast, Marilyn Miller, Rhoda Otto

Ingredients:

- 1 ½ cups butter, softened
- 2 ¼ cups brown sugar
- ¾ cup sugar
- 3 (3 oz.) packages instant vanilla pudding
- 1 Tbsp. baking soda
- 6 eggs
- 1 Tbsp. vanilla
- 6 ¾ cups flour
- 1 (11 oz.) package chocolate chips

Instructions:
Mix in order given. Dough will be stiff.
Make balls and roll in sugar. Flatten with fork or hand.
Bake at 350–375°F.
Do not bake until brown—just lightly tinted.

"A great deal of what we see depends on what we are looking for."
—*Amish Proverb*

Recipe book holder in an Amish kitchen

14

The Rural Bus Driver's Trip to the Chiropractor

The life of an Amish driver was never predictable. Having recently returned home, I reflected on the past week's memorable trip to Wisconsin. I wondered when the next call would come. Who would it come from? And where would we be going?

A couple of days later, the next three calls came like three exciting blasts from a horn. One came from a man wanting me to haul him in my pick-up truck to Menards for supplies. Another came from a man asking me to drive him and a van full of others to an auction in Southern Iowa. And the last call came from a man asking me to drive him and others to Lebanon, Iowa for a chiropractor appointment.

As a child I'd dreamed of being a mother, of being a nurse, and of traveling to far away first world destinations to teach and uplift others. Never in my wildest childhood dreams did I imagine getting out of bed at all hours of the night and with my young daughter as my companion, pick up simply dressed religious people I'd never met before to take them on a trip, anywhere in the country, using my personal vehicle. That's what I found myself doing for a living, and loving it!

The following morning Violet and I drove to Blaire to pick up Lester Fry and his wife Ester who were both strangers to me. Before heading to Lebanon for the Chiropractor appointment, Lester instructed me to pick up his son Irvine, his wife Saloma and their two young children. That did not surprise me because the Amish always like other passengers to go along. However, they often don't tell you when they call.

Lester, short, with a large nose, and dirty gray blue clothing, opened the van's back doors and placed within a large box of home-grown tomatoes. He then walked to the passenger side, climbed up and seated himself in the seat next to me. His wife settled in the seat behind us. With a "hello", and a "let's go" we were off to pick up the other passengers.

Driving around the community of about sixty-five families spread over twenty or so miles, I suddenly became the rural bus driver. With a ready smile, Lester directed me to stop at several homes where some people got into my van. At the next stop some got out. At the next stop others got in and then we went back to where we dropped some off to pick them up again. I began to understand the job of a school bus driver. I was glad they knew what was going on and where they were going because I sure didn't.

Fully loaded, chit-chat from several ongoing conversations filled the airspace of the van. Shortly after crossing the Iowa boarder Lester turned to me requesting I stop in Sweet Home at the Casey's Gas Station and General Store. We were still rolling when the van's three side doors flew open and my passengers descended upon the Casey's. Violet and I stayed in the van wondering what all the fuss was about. One person ran to the back of the van to get something out, a few others dashed into the store.

Ester, her long legs carrying her tall wide frame, headed to the right side of the store. I thought that was odd because there was no store entrance along that side. After just a moment, she returned making her way to the rear passenger entry of the van. A smile lit up her face, her eyes shining with victory. Her strong, dirty arm stretched out toward me holding a very full fifty-five-gallon black bag of trash, the outside dripping with a light brown odiferous liquid.

Turning to look at her, eyebrows raised, I pointed to the trash bag questioning, "Where did you get that?"

Still smiling, as though nothing were unusual about the situation, she pointed ahead and to the right responding, "Over there against the wall."

Looking at her with confusion mixed with horror, I asked her, "Why are you putting that smelly, stinky, dirty Casey's trash bag in my van?"

She replied with a 'humph' as though that were a dumb question, "There is dog food in it." In my mind, I saw dog food cans, bags of doggy treats and dry dog food in paper bags. Knowing Casey's didn't sell such dog food, I asked Ester, "What kind of dog food?"

"Pizza, chicken and donuts mostly." she responded, again, as though I as wasting her time in asking such dumb questions.

Taking in a deep breath to gather my thoughts, not knowing how to handle that situation, being new at driving taxi for the Amish, I allowed it. I didn't want that dirty, smelly bag of stale rotting food in the van at all, yet there it was. I instructed Ester to please put it in the back. She placed the trash bag in the back of the van next to the box of plump, juicy, fresh from the garden red tomatoes. It was 100 °F outside with 90% humidity and you can imagine what that garbage bag was going to do.

We and our smelly new traveling companion, made our way to the chiropractor after that. Upon arriving Ester left the trash to cook at 172 °F for an hour and a half in my sweltering van. Violet, pink teddy bear rolling backpack in tow, and I followed the Amish into the chiropractor's office to wait in the coolness of the air-conditioned building.

We were invited into the back waiting room with the Amish. While waiting, one of my passengers, a sweet young mother named Saloma, offered to braid Violet's hair the Amish way. I watched closely hoping to learn to braid her hair in that fashion on my own. Braiding done, Violet took her littlest pet shop figures out of her backpack and played quietly while I read from a magazine. Hearing the doctor and Amish conversing across the room, I looked up to see a trade going on. The Amish were trading the tomatoes for their treatments; at least for part of their treatments. As a city girl, I did not understand that barter and trade still existed in the real world.

Within an hour and a half, all nine of the Amish had completed their treatments and returned to the van. Violet and I left the cool comfort of the doctor's office for the van before everyone arrived. Opening the van door, we were greeted by the odor of rotting meat invading our nostrils. It was so strong it made us want to retch. Reaching for the spray bottle with a mixture of peppermint essential oil and water that I kept on hand to keep the van smelling good, I immediately and thoroughly sprayed the interior of van, including the garbage bag. The ride home would have been intolerable otherwise.

"Dr. Swedberg was a unique kind of chiropractor," Lester, a man in his mid-fifties and bishop of the Amish church, informed me on the way home. He was in a talkative mood. "While I was a young man while tearing down a home, the second story wall fell on me. At that time, I didn't go to the doctor, believing nothing was seriously amiss. However, after a few days I wasn't coping so I took a trip to the chiropractor. A disk was knocked out of place and needed correcting. Since then, I've had to make regular trips to the chiropractor to keep things in place. Once in a while I'll do something to completely knock it out again, as I did yesterday while working with the hogs," he explained, informing me of the need for his trip to the chiropractor that day.

Continuing on down the interstate, I heard the sound of a cooler being opened, rustling plastic and the pop of a lid coming off a can. The smell of homemade bread, canned meat, and fresh lettuce filled the van. Ester was making sandwiches for everyone's noon meal.

Done with their sandwiches, they requested I make a stop at Casey's. I was hesitant to do so, mortified at the thought that Ester would get another dirty, smelly garbage bag to place in the back of my van; more dog food.

"Here we go again I thought." However, they just wanted to get soda pop and soft serve ice cream. As a general rule the Amish LOVED ice cream.

Traveling through Sweet Home, Iowa, Lester asked that we stop at Wal-Mart. I was happy to do it, knowing how traveling in the van afforded them the opportunity to run errands they couldn't otherwise run. Further along, they directed me off the highway to a thrift shop just over the Missouri border. Sadly, it was closed.

We finally arrived in Blaire to drop people off, nearing the end of my exhausting bus driving day. The first stop was Elmer and Sylvia's home. Tallying up the total, the Amish asked me to divide the number by nine, which brought each person's bill to $28.50. I rounded it down to $28.00 each. They were good people. That group, though, was among the poorer in the community.

Next to be dropped off was Ruben T's daughter. Before leaving, I purchased a gallon of raw milk from him. Seizing the moment Violet jumped out of the van to chase his chickens that were scurrying all over the yard. She loved chickens and actually caught one! Lester, Ester and the dirty, smelly trash bag were dropped off next, to our great relief. Lastly, we stopped at Dave Chupp's to drop our remaining passenger off. While there I purchased seven dozen eggs and we were finally free to go home.

Each time I went to Amish country, even if it was not on personal business but to haul them, it was like a vortex. Hours would be spent there running people here and there, visiting, and waiting. Traveling down State Highway S on the return home, we came upon a buggy carrying two men and a blue heeler dog who was sitting behind them enjoying the view from the open buggy doors. I was forced to slow down a bit until we crested the hill and it was safe to pass. As I sped home after having spent hours with the horrible baking bag of trash in the rear of my van, my thoughts were consumed with getting out of those now dirty and smelly clothes we were wearing. How nice it would be to take a long, hot soapy shower and put fresh, clean clothing on; thus, ending our day with our slow paced, simple Amish friends.

I could hardly wait for the next time.

"Contentment is not getting what we want but being satisfied with what we have." —*Amish Proverb*

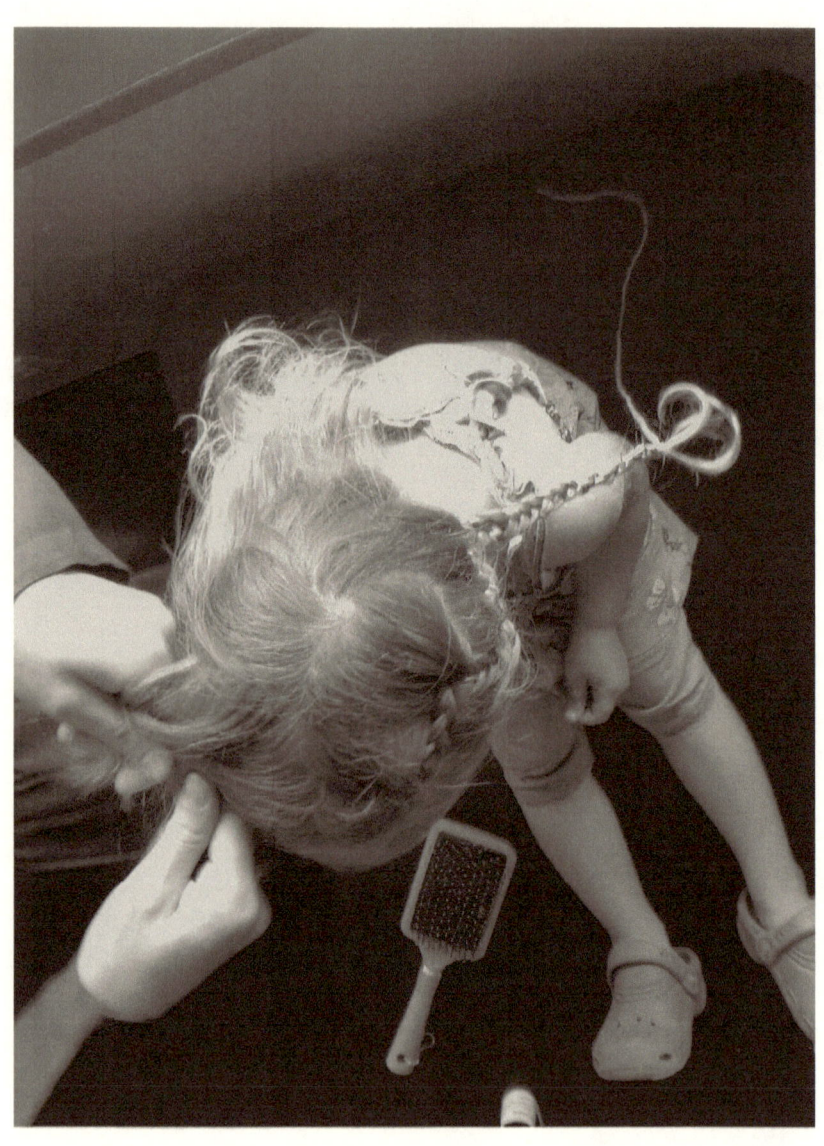

Violet having her hair braided the Amish way

15

Driving Someone New

The short-trilled sound of cicadas 'chirr, chirr, chirr chirping', the tweet, tweet, tweet of birds singing, and the haha, ahaha, haha of children's laughter filled the outdoor spaces of our tiny Missouri town announcing the beginning of summer. That early June afternoon the children and I enjoyed a playful day at the swimming pool; a nice reprieve from the blistering hot sun. While taking a break my phone rang. It was the bishop's wife, Naomi of Blaire. She was calling to confirm our upcoming Minnesota and Wisconsin trip, and she also asked me to discount my rates because the van would be nearly empty. Only four people would be going along instead of the original six. Being still new to private driving, and perhaps a bit of a pushover, I agreed on the condition that she give me raw honey from one of her many beehives, enough to make up for how much I discount the trip. She happily agreed.

Gasp! Ahh ha ha! Just as we were in the midst of our conversation, I heard several pool patrons gasping, some laughing, others screaming.

A large frog made its way across the lawn, through the cyclone fence, across the concrete that surrounded the pool and jumped in for a swim, frightening the children and causing the life guards to jump into action to remove the intruding amphibian. Situation and noise back under control I returned to my conversation with Naomi, letting her know I would be heading to Blaire later that day to tend to business there. Before transporting new passengers, I liked to find their house and meet them to discuss details and let them see my van.

A small framed older woman came out of the front door of her one-story ranch style home, walking barefoot across the gray Berber rug of her patio to greet me; she lifted her heart shaped porcelain face toward me in a kindly resolute gesture. In hand she carried a list of several other drivers. Next to their names in neat print were the prices they charged. All said drivers were already booked, and some ran quite cheap, one at just $0.50 per mile for a seven passenger van Naomi informed me, hoping to make her case stronger for my lowering my prices. Ignoring that comment because we had already made a deal, I replied, "we had already agreed upon this, I'd discount my price, and you would give me honey for the difference." As some of the very conservative Amish did not recognize daylight savings time, she informed me that I would be picking them up at midnight her time, which meant 1:00 a.m. my time. That was confusing.

Before leaving, Naomi filled bags with fresh picked radishes and lettuce from her garden for me to take home and share with my family.

My next stop was to Ester's home where I would purchase raw milk, then to Sylvia's country store for some dried goods. It was funny because as I was running around debating if I should go back to Naomi's to ask for permission to take my son on the trip, in addition to taking my daughter, which she had already agreed to, divine providence intervened.

While heading down the gravel road to Sylvia's, I came upon an older Amish man driving his buggy who frantically waved me down indicating for me to stop my van. His appearance was similar to others with his gray stringy beard, long, wrinkled face, and partially toothless grin. I'd never seen the man before. He happened to be the other guy, Toby, who also would be traveling with us on Sunday. He asked me to take him to see Naomi and David.

What a strange situation. I was flagged down by a man I'd never met before, asking me for a ride, and I happily gave it to him. In my world as a city girl never would I have dreamed of giving a ride to somebody I didn't know; it would have been reckless and dangerous. And there I was agreeing to that, how my world was changing. It occurred to me that I was picking up an Amish hitchhiker.

Toby confidently placed himself in the front seat of my van and began talking my ear off. He smiled continually, and was quite a witty man, an enjoyable person to be around. I asked him if it was okay to bring not only Violet along on the trip, but Jack as well. He had no problem with it since there was plenty of room. We checked in with Naomi and her husband David, they had no problem either. That was an answer to my prayers. My family found it tough when I left Jack at home during my travels. He was a very active child, picking on the other children and getting into mischief. With him coming along we could spend quality time together. Besides, he hadn't traveled with me since my first trip with the Amish at Christmas time. We were both excited to include him on this trip.

"Daylight saving time is based on the ancient idea of lengthening a blanket by cutting off one end and seeing it on the other end."
—*A Native American chief*

Amish barn built with corrugated tin from old hog pens

16

A Wild Nights Drive

I should have paid attention to my brain instead of my heart and just gotten up to get things done, because my mind, racing with needless concerns about our upcoming trip with the Amish would not allow my body to rest that night. At church the next morning several people informed me of how tired they felt I looked. That afternoon I laid down for three hours in the 95°F temperature, with 80% humidity, hoping to get much needed sleep before driving the Amish all night. No luck, again, sleep eluded me. Picking the Amish up at 1:00 a.m., (midnight their time) going into driving that night would be a challenge.

It was always difficult locating Amish homes after sunset because they lived in the country with no electricity. If there was a light on in the home, it was battery, propane, or kerosene powered, thus, very dim. Thankfully I'd found David and Naomi's house in the previous daylight, which made it easier for me to find when using only the light of the moon and stars. Pulling into their drive, David and Naomi, neither of whom was wearing shoes, promptly came out of their home, bags in hand and boarded the van. They instructed me to drive to another Amish man's house because he might have wanted to go with us. That was the first I'd heard of him. Amish were known to do that; add people to the load without prior notice. It turned out that man wasn't going to be going after all. Next, we picked up Toby and his wife Lucy and then were on our way, Toby my companion in the front, my two children Violet and Jack on the bench behind me.

"Deer!" warned Toby, pointing to our left as we traveled down the two-lane state highway going into Iowa. There was a doe, on the shoulder, rocking back and forth on her hind legs debating on if she could beat my van. Without conscious thought my foot gently put pressure on the brake so as to not hit her. About thirty miles into Iowa heading north on the interstate blue and red flashing lights broke up the dark highway ahead of us. We came upon massive amounts of sticky matter, scarlet blood splattered all over the freeway, crossing both lanes, intermixed with pieces of light brown fur, and large chunks of viscous, garish flesh. An enormous buck lay on its side, white underbelly exposed, blood draining from his mouth in scarlet strings, his hind end torn off and lying dead on the side of the road. Up ahead on the shoulder stood a man with a worried look on his face, nervously pacing back and forth next to his severely damaged brand-new pick-up truck. He had just hit that deer. Massive winged vultures, with focused eyes, and ready claws swooped down, barely missing my windshield to waste no time devouring the fresh kill, surely a welcome treat. As we continued through the night several possums, raccoons, and rabbits darted in front of the van startling me along the way. Wildlife was out in droves that evening, perhaps due to the full moon. How grateful we were to have made it to our destination safely and without harming any wildlife despite its unusual amounts of activity that night.

Both hands on the steering wheel, my right leg propped up on the driver's seat under my left leg, looking straight ahead, eyes glazed over, neck doing its best to keep my head up, I succumbed to overwhelming feelings of drowsiness. My head dropped occasionally, then it would snap back, eyes desperately wanting to close as I zoned out; it was difficult to stay awake and alert through the night. Around 4:00 a.m. it became even more difficult to continue driving, pulling over to sleep would have been a better option. Everyone in the van was sleeping. We made it though. By the time we arrived, I'd been up for twenty-four hours. I wondered why we couldn't leave at 6:00 p.m. the previous night instead of driving all night. It seemed driving all night would be hard on everyone; it sure was hard on me. Most of us are taught that Sunday was a day of rest, and the Amish abided by that by not traveling on Sundays unless under extenuating circumstances such as emergency or death.

Going into that trip Toby didn't have any plans. He would improvise when we got there. We arrived in Talent, Iowa at about 8:00 a.m. where Toby arbitrarily picked an Amish house to stop at. As if he knew the homeowners and would get exactly what he wanted, Toby boldly knocked on their front door and invited his group to stay there for the day, which they were allowed to do. It was decided best to find another location for us Englischers. Toby back in the van directed me to drive to someone else's house. Again, he confidently knocked on the door and asked if we could stay there for the day. They said yes, invited us in and showed us their guest room. I felt very uncomfortable not staying with the group we came with. Enos and his wife Lydia, our hosts, spent the day at church services (Amish hold church on Sundays, but when there is a wedding or funeral, they also hold church services) leaving us there by ourselves; which was even more unusual. Lydia ran a dry goods and grocery store and invited me to take care of the customers as they would surely arrive. What a strange request, she was asking me, a complete stranger to take on that responsibility, and trusting me to do it. I refused, so exhausted was I, desperately needing a nap. The bed we were kindly offered obviously hadn't had the sheets changed. Pulling back the bedding revealed long strands of hair and fresh brown stains. I felt a twinge of disgust, as I was from the city and we always kept fresh sheets on the beds, especially if guests were going to be sleeping in them, though Enos and Lydia had no idea guests were coming. As country folk did back in the day, and as many

81

Amish then, one day a week was set aside especially for wash, so if the sheets got soiled, they'd stay that way till wash day. I was reminded of the children's rhyme.

Wash on Monday,
Iron on Tuesday,
Mend on Wednesday,
Churn on Thursday,
Clean on Friday,
Bake on Saturday,
Rest on Sunday.

We were too tired to care about the dirty bed. Violet and I lay down while Jack stayed up and was served a wonderful breakfast of cereal and milk, fresh strawberries, eggs and carrots before the family went to church.

After three hours of solid sleep, I woke up. Jack was not in the house, though evidence that he had been there getting into mischief was abundant in the matches left on surfaces, scissors sitting out, and glass everywhere. Leaving Violet sleeping, I quietly slipped outside to find Jack, who was in the chicken house, barefoot, strong little arms concealed in the downy brown feathers of the very perturbed hen he was holding. Yep, he was doing something he wasn't supposed to be, but at least he didn't burn the house down. Upon finding him, we returned to the house to clean up the mess.

"Quick, let's pick up before our hosts return, quick!" Bending over glass I directed Jack to gather every match and return scissors to their place. That evening we were fortunate to have a sit-down dinner with the family. The dining table, eight foot long, made of dark polished wood, with benches on either side was set with simple stainless steel metal bowls and cups, forks and knives, no napkins, and no table cloth. As was Amish tradition, the men sat on one side of the table with women and children on the other. Dinner was a pasta dish I'd seen several times already, thin rectangular noodles with small pieces of meat lathered in a creamy sauce. There was a salad made with cream of some sort, eggs, and a dark green leafy substance, topped with cheese, it did not appear to be healthy at all, but at least there was a little green. There were soda crackers, a pile of homemade wheat bread on a plate, with apple butter or butter for a spread. Everyone having cleaned their bowls nearly spotless; dessert was placed at the table to be eaten next. It was a dense sweet cake served with strawberries and/or milk over the top. We prayed silently before supper, then after supper as was the Amish way when non-Amish guests were at their table. They prayed in silence.

After the amazing supper I was stuffed and ready to nap again; however, that wasn't how being a driver worked. We got back into the van under the guidance of Toby. My passengers napped while I drove them to Lafayette, Iowa to drop off David and Lucy, then to Minnesota, just across the border to return Lamar. He had been dropped off for church earlier in the day. I was his ride home. Then we traveled to King City, Iowa to Elmer's house where we would spend the next night. We arrived there at about 12:30 a.m.; it was another late night. As we climbed the wooden steps onto the front porch, leading into the house, Violet, Jack and I heard a low growl from under the porch. It was the family dog and he didn't like strangers. What a fitting end to a crazy day!

"Firewood heats you twice – once when you cut it and again when you burn it." —*Amish Proverb*

Enclosed staircase typical in many Amish homes

17

The Amish are Human too

Uo ist yesus mein verlangen; what a wonderful way to fall into a peaceful, happy sleep. Rap tap tap, rap tap tap, rap tap tap, the sound at 4:00 a.m. rudely jolted me out of my restful sleep. It was Toby waking me up to drive everyone to the wedding in Wisconsin that dark, cool Wednesday morning. It was a three-hour trip to Jefferson and I was tired, still not recovered from the trip thus far. We weren't the only ones up at that crazy hour; within a five mile stretch of highway right on the Iowa/Minnesota border we saw six deer, a raccoon and a couple of pheasants. Watching the sky as it turned from black to brilliant yellows, oranges, and pinks as night turned to day just about made it worth getting up early. It certainly made for a more pleasant trip; because I was only ever up that early when hauling Amish. We crossed the Mississippi River, just as the bright golden sun crested the horizon. Lovely!

At about 7:30 a.m. we arrived at Toby's sister's home nestled in the hills with majestic pines. There we were served a breakfast of cereal, milk and strawberries. After breakfast we continued on to the wedding. Arms loaded with wedding gifts of silver bowls and cleaning supplies; my passengers hurried from the van. After dropping the wedding guests off, the children and I returned to Toby's sister's house to nap. Typical of how Toby operated, I didn't know if we'd drive home all night or stop three hours away to spend the night at Elmer's house again. Whatever their plans were, I needed to be prepared. Toby's sister showed me around the house inviting us to pick whatever beds we'd like and make ourselves at home and then she left for the wedding. Violet and I chose a double bed in the living room; Jack chose what must have been a boy's bedroom, to sleep in. I prayed in my heart if Jack got up he'd be respectful of their property. We had a talk about what he could do while we napped. Jack didn't sleep at all; I woke up to him playing in the wash room sink, water running onto the floor, sink filled with bubbles from the hand soap. He'd scribbled in the guest book that was lying open on the dining room table, and Violet, who also woke up before I did, informed me that Jack threw rocks at a horse. Good thing I hid the scissors that were out in the open on the table; who knows what he would have done had he found those. Apparently, Jack wasn't tired, he was bored.

Hungry and knowing supper was served at the wedding we headed there. Upon arriving we were greeted by the wedding hosts and ushered into the basement to dine at a colorful table covered in scrumptious dishes; barbecued meat patties, bologna sandwiches, mashed potatoes, potato salad and desserts of Jell-O, fruit, and a divine peanut butter and chocolate pie. I could have eaten a LOT more of that!

After supper Jack and Violet headed outside to play with the other children. Done eating, I came upstairs, headed outside and spotted Jack cowering under a spruce tree, trash surrounding him, and a handful of small Amish boys laughing in his direction. Concerned, I walked over to see if he was okay; he assured me he was. Meanwhile Violet played on the tree swing surrounded by about fifteen little girls. Feeling my children were okay, with time on my hands, I went to sit in the van to calculate the trip thus far. Shortly thereafter, Jack ran up to me, nearly in tears, informing me the Amish boys were teasing him, throwing stuff at him and laughing at him. Sensitive of his situation, I hugged him and gently reminded him that he had been unkind to others in the past, inviting him to remember that feeling when tempted to be unkind in the future. A few minutes later I heard Violet cry while sitting on the swing, her hands concealing her face in frustration. Releasing Jack, I went to her to find several girls throwing grass at her. They apparently wanted to swing and Violet wouldn't give it up. I carried a sweet crying little girl to my van, cleaned her off and asked how else she could spend her time. She and Jack agreed to go back and play in the sand box that was unoccupied at that moment. No sooner were they settled in playing, than they were surrounded by another large crowd of children. Thinking it a good idea to keep a closer eye on my children I got my laptop out of the van, found a spot to sit leaning against a clothes line and got to work typing.

Within a few moments I was surrounded by little ones too, curious at what I was doing. Tired of the sandbox Violet got her pink backpack out so she could play with her toys. The Amish children were very interested. At first, they intently watched as Violet took each item out one by one, a pet shop animal, a purple plastic horse, a plastic piece of pizza, a plastic carrot, a few books, and a Magna Doodle. She showed the children each toy and generously handed them out to share. All that activity caught the attention of a couple of mothers, who briskly strode over to their children, their manners heavy with animosity, firmly speaking in Pennsylvania Deutsch discouraging them from playing with Violet's toys. The Amish children were hustled away. Oblivious, my children played on happily. Moving on to other things, my children left their toys in the grass, to be later discovered by a few teenage boys. They took particular interest in the Magna Doodle jokingly writing messages on it, hanging it from the cloths line and a tree laughing and having a good time. Later on, I got report from Jack that those same little boys who'd previously teased him were being cruel, trying to destroy Violet's pink backpack. I found it sitting next to the clothesline, covered in grass. I realized then they were actually jealous of my children's possessions because they had toys that the Amish children weren't allowed to have. That explained their behavior.

After dinner there was a lull in activity at the house. Buggies and van loads of people left to go home and "chore" as the Amish said. The man of the home where the wedding was held was very kind to seek Jack out leading him across the lane to introduce Jack to his Holstein calves. They were in housed a small round metal pen. He gave Jack a very large bottle of milk to feed a calf with. For Jack that was a new experience. Excited, the calf put his front legs up on the metal piping to get better access; Jack allowed the calf, with its long pink tongue to lick his fingers in search for the bottle nipple. A few minutes later he came running to me reporting the calf bit him, yet it really grazed his fingers with her teeth. Yet he had a smile on his face, thrilled by the new experience.

Those little Amish boys must have gotten bored again, because once again they surrounded my son taunting him. That time he ran to the van to find me and the boys followed, continuing with their jeering. Jack, nearly in tears, refused to be comforted by my open arms, and refused to fight back. Looking directly in the boys' eyes, with sternness in my voice I ordered them to leave my boy alone; they went away. After a few moments, Jack and Violet, together, bravely went back to the main yard to play...again.

Settled back in my van working on bookkeeping, a young couple, faces glowing, gliding blissfully along, obviously courting, approached my driver's side door asking if they could sit in my van. Thinking they wanted to get out of the heat and away from the dirt and insects outside I responded "Okay" before fully realizing what I'd just agreed to. Another driver, an older gentleman, sat in his van across the lane, killing time by playing on his phone. I thought to myself that perhaps he might be more experienced than me in such matters. Concerned at what I'd just permitted, I made my way to his driver's side door and knocked on the window. He rolled it down. I introduced myself, wasting no time in reporting to him what I'd just allowed. "Am I aiding and abetting forbidden behavior?" I asked him, concern in my voice. "Am I going to get in trouble from the Amish elders?" Just then peering into the back of his van I spotted a young couple sitting together on the rear bench, one being Rosanna, a girl of about twenty that we were staying with in Iowa. They were listening to what was going on between the driver and me, finding my questions and comments quite humorous. From the back Rosanna and her sweetheart assured me "it's just fine." After Rosanna and her sweetheart exited the van the driver, Ronald advised me not to tell anyone about it cautioning me to "let the young people be young people." Wow, that was totally unexpected I thought to myself; more "on the job training".

Continuing the eventful day, Elmer found me. He needed to pick up the shoes he left at his sister's house. Jack and Violet stayed at the wedding while I took Elmer. Traveling along I told him of Jack's experience being bullied. Upset by what I reported he assured me, "That behavior is unacceptable." Shortly after returning that same group of boys sought Jack out and loaded his hands with candy. They showed him kindness the rest of the evening. Things improved for Violet and the girls, too. Elmer must have done some nosing around and talking with parents. It was so appreciated.

Dusk set in, coloring the sky orange and brown, making way for the moon to shine. Meanwhile, I sat in the van watching the happenings outside. Violet and her group of about fifteen followers positioned themselves near the van visiting with one another. The next thing I heard was a loud Bwahaha, bwahaha, bwahah coming from outside my van. Bewildered, I hopped out. A particular girl, obviously the oldest and seeming designated spokesperson reported that a kitten sprinted under the van and without another thought Violet threw herself onto the gravel driveway, and on all fours scurried under the van to the other side to catch the kitten, to which the kitten sprinted under the van again and so did Violet, eventually catching it. At that uproarious laughter escaped from the Amish girls, tears of laughter streamed down their faces. That was some entertainment for those girls. Wish I could have seen that!

The evening wore on, seemingly endlessly. Since my children were faring well, I made my way to visit with three other drivers who were standing in a circle outside their vans. One, a middle-aged man chewing tobacco and drinking pop, was on disability because he had an accident while driving cement truck. The second driver a blond haired slightly overweight middle-aged woman, owned a fleet of vans and hired other drivers to drive for her. The third driver, an overweight bald man, drove to make a living. Introductions over, still learning and always open to new ideas on how to improve my driving, I asked them for tips on how to stay awake all night while driving. The tobacco chewing driver suggested...chewing tobacco to stay awake, the substantially overweight driver purchased caffeine pills, kept them in front of his van for use as needed, and the female driver used energy drinks. That was no help to me as what I was really hoping for was natural solutions.

After a late supper of hotdogs and beans, potatoes and cheese and pasta salad I watched the children play in the yard while the young people visited. Men's low, chant like singing floated from the house while clattering dishes and moving furniture could be heard from the women cleaning up the kitchen. With my stomach settled, ready for dessert I headed into the basement, where I was greeted by about two hundred wedding guests, all in their best clothing, the women in black dresses with white aprons, black halz düchs,° (or called capes in in English), and white kapps, men in their black slacks and white shirts. They sat at folding tables adorned in beautiful glassware in an assortment of bright colors; bowls full of decadent desserts down the center. Standing in front of everyone at a table with the wedding party were the newlyweds. I was surprised to see the wedding couple's attire to be different from the usual Amish dress. The groom wore black slacks and a white shirt instead of his traditional muted colors, and the bride sewed herself a new dress in her favorite color, which would also serve as a church dress, and the clothing she'd be buried in. Standing there, groom with a knife in hand, ready to cut their fancy white three-tiered wedding cake dotted in simple purple iced flowers.

Standing at the landing, I quickly turned around to head back upstairs so as to not disturb the party, when a sweet lady touched my arm, asked what I wanted and led me to the dessert table. Heading back up the stairs, chocolate pie in hand I thought to myself, "The Amish surprisingly do have similar wedding traditions as us non-Amish."

Festivities over, it was time to head home. My passengers loaded up and we headed out. It was only a three-hour drive to Elmer and Ester's, but I was tired. My struggle to stay awake was real, so it was a blessing to stay in Iowa for the night before heading home. As we traveled down back roads in the evening's darkness, I was losing it; the van's vibration on the gravel road relaxed me, lulling me to sleep resulting in my head falling to my shoulder and eyes closing. Had the night's trip been longer, I would have pulled over to nap, but we were almost there so we continued; I kept jerking myself awake. No one seemed to notice my trouble driving because they were all sleeping. I scared myself pretty badly that evening. Obviously, I needed some help in staying awake during night driving.

Miraculously we made it safely to Elmer and Ester's. My children and I almost stayed in the van to sleep; it took all I had to get us into the house and settled into the guest bedroom.

A Knock, knock, knock on my door at 6:30 my time (5:30 their time, that community didn't observe day light savings) woke me out of my deep slumber. Still drained, sleep could have continued on for hours, yet the Amish needed me up; it was time to get going. Ester served us a delicious breakfast of meat patties, fried eggs and apple sauce. Toby invited the children and me to participate in morning devotional which was held after right after breakfast. He let me know it would be in German and a prayer would be offered on bended knee, but we didn't have to kneel for the prayer if we didn't want to. Grateful for the opportunity, I thanked him; informing him we too had morning devotions with scripture and prayer as a family, so that was nothing unusual for us. When the boys returned to the house from their morning choring we began. The women placed the dining room chairs in a circle to the right of the table. We each sat on a chair while Toby, leaning on his chair on bended knee, with his right hand resting on the seat, small black book in hand, in a deep, chanting like voice read scriptures in German Ich bin klein mein herz ist rein soll niemond darin wohnen als Yesus allein. We were then instructed to kneel, resting our arms on our chair seat, while Toby, using the same deep chanting voice, offered a humble prayer in Pennsylvania Deutsch Wir danken dir, himmilscher vater, durch yescena Christem unsern herrn fur diese genossen gaben und alle deine wohlthaten, der bu lebst und regierest in ewigkeit Amen. With the prayer over everyone quickly got up and was off to work again, the ladies and young girls finishing dishes, and the men and boys to tend to the animals in the barn. I was off to work too, loading up the van for our trip home.

Van loaded; I returned to the house to discover Violet wearing an Amish kapp. Rosanna (the same girl sitting in the back of driver Ronald's van) went up to the attic and got it for her as a gift. It used to be hers when she was a three-year-old; her mother made it for her. What a sweet gesture; that was a gift my little Violet will treasure always. A few minutes later Violet and Jack were running around the Livingroom/dining room chasing rubber bouncy balls. Ester bashfully confessed; she bought the balls for the children as a gift. Again, my heart was warmed. Ester took my children under her wing as if they were her own, sharing with me that she'd like to keep

Violet and Jack too as her own children. I give Ester a warm hug, and thanked her for her and her family's kindness; no words could express my feelings. Violet and Jack also hugged Ester, Jack then said goodbye to her young boys, his new friends, and we were off.

Of all the places we've stayed thus far Elmer and Ester's house was my favorite. There was SO much love and goodness there; it was difficult to leave the warmth of that home.

"The person who sows seeds of kindness will have a perpetual harvest."
—*Amish Proverb*

Jack and Violet outside an Amish home

18

Driving the Business

I'd been home for two weeks after an extended vacation to visit family. Prior to that trip, I'd only hauled Amish for four months. Upon returning I had two previously arranged hauling jobs, both with the same family to the same location, and both for weddings. Knowing there was a new driver on the scene, and that people may have forgotten about me, I sought answers by visiting my dear Amish friend David M.

Saloma, David M's wife, typical of most Amish women, took her household and childcare duties very seriously, so seriously, in fact, she didn't even notice I'd been invited into the house by David. I sat with him at his twelve-foot-long homemade dining room table to discuss my business, while Saloma, whom I didn't even notice at first either, was to our left on her hands and knees at the cookstove cleaning it.

David informed me that the new gal, Tina, whom also had a large van, was quite popular as a driver. Her popularity, along with my long-term absence concerned me as I wanted to get back into driving and drive full time. David shared with me the same wisdom he shared with Tina, who, too had come to him for guidance.

To me he counseled, "Now, the Amish don't want to pay a whole lot for haulers, they are poor and it can get real expensive, Okay?"

"Okay," I replied. "

You might want to consider lowering your prices a bit. You see, the Amish will call the cheapest first, and go from there."

"It doesn't matter what the van, car, or truck looks or runs like, the Amish just want to get there and cheaply."

"In light of that, now, I don't want to tell you what to do, but it wouldn't hurt to lower your prices a little bit." He continued.

"Okay," I said, not liking what he was saying, but keeping that to myself.

"I've been doing numbers, please help me, to be sure they are accurate and that I'm still making a profit." I requested of him.

He got up, walked across the dining room to a desk, grabbed a pencil and paper and started doing the numbers. He figured I could make $0.50 profit per mile running my twelve-passenger van at $0.75, and my truck at $0.70, which in his mind, was decent money. I was very skeptical with the numbers he gave me as they did not account for wear and tear and maintenance, nor insurance. I sat there pondering his advice while he continued.

After running numbers, and settling on prices David advised me to print out two hundred business cards and distribute them to surrounding communities, especially since two of the communities didn't even have one driver with a large van.

Explaining himself, he added "You see, Amish men, we collect business cards. We like to keep them in our wallet and when we need a driver, we pull our pile of cards out and start calling, just one after the other till we get a driver." He continued.

Knowing me and how I was one of the rare Englischers who didn't keep their phone attached at the hip, he added, "If the driver doesn't answer the phone, we move on to the next one. It's inconvenient for us to leave a message and wait for a driver to call us back. You must always have your phone with you, and answer if it's Amish calling."

Armed with new information, and filled with gratitude for David's guidance and sincere desire to help me be successful, I got in my truck to take the fifteen-minute drive back to my home.

My best chance at success in passing out cards was to have an Amish man come along with me I figured. My friend David P agreed to assist me in exchange for a free ride to his parents' home in one of the communities we'd be visiting.

One chilly October Friday morning, with new cards and flyers in hand, I was ready to go. My four-year-old Violet and I picked David P up and we headed off. First, we delivered cards to his community, to which he volunteered to hand out for me. Generally, the Amish were very social people; I thought to myself that perhaps David P wanted to have reason to visit with his community members? No matter, I very much appreciated his assistance. The next community we visited, Blaire, was a thirty-minute drive away. David directed me where to stop, enthusiastically jumping out of the truck and handing out my cards, while catching up with his Blaire friends too.

With the Blaire Community flooded with my business cards David directed me to our first stop in Iowa, the little town of Warren a few miles north of the Missouri border. Along the way we passed through Bandon, Iowa, also another Amish community. Passing the Bandon Country Store, I pointed it out, telling David I wished there were a similar store in one of the communities closer to us. At that, David piped up, "I think I'd like to stop in." We turned around and made an impromptu stop at the store. David had always been very open with me, sharing information most Englischers weren't privy to. That situation was no different as he told me about the Warren Country Store owners Fannie Mae and Delbert Burkholder. They recently left the church due to disputes and have since been dealt with, in his opinion, unfairly.

Responding, I informed him, "I remember going to the store several months ago, the woman behind the counter was dressed Amish, and at least one or two other Amish women were working in the store. That must be a recent development."

"It is" David confirmed, adding, "I know some of their relatives. Their leaving was a point of tension within the family, a taboo subject."

"I'll keep it between us" I assured him.

While David P had a lively conversation with Fannie Mae, Violet and I shopped. A book, The Happening: Nickle Mines School Tragedy by Harvey Yoder caught my eye. I brought it up to the counter for purchasing, and was invited to join in the conversation. Fannie Mae, still living in her home and running her store in the community, reported that when they left the church in February members of the community told them "We won't shun you, but we just can't associate with you anymore." She felt people had been less than kind; they stopped patronizing her store leaving her with several thousands in Amish specific merchandise to deal with.

Half smiling, and tilting her head "Business has been good in other ways though," she reported optimistically.

My heart broke for her and her family. I could tell she suffered and was a good woman. Continuing on a few miles north of Warren we arrived in Aurora. David P directed me to the bishop's house where he got out, and handed him a pile of my cards, since Aurora had no store, he figured the bishop could hand them out. Our last stop was Hillsboro, Iowa, about an hour's drive East of Aurora. The only stop we made there was David's parents' home, as his dad was the bishop of the community.

The Hillsboro Amish community had a history of families coming and going; the community was down to just four families at one recent point, now it was back up to about sixteen and growing. There wasn't yet a community store. Violet and I were invited into David's parents' home. David dined and visited with his loved ones while Violet and I made ourselves comfortable in a corner of the large kitchen/dining room/living room. David's mom Sarah, a very sweet, short and plump lady in her late sixties came to visit with me. She settled in a rocking chair across from me openly speaking of her family, how she had birthed eleven children; seven boys and four girls, three of whom were passed on already. One boy died due to a heart condition at age twenty, another boy to a tumor in his late thirties, and a girl as a young child who was born with physical challenges. In her mind, she lost a fourth child, due to his leaving the family, as she put it. He left the Amish to live the English life. Once in a while her son visited and surprisingly Sarah seemed to accept it, whereas some Amish wouldn't allow it, cutting off all contact, pretending the child was dead. In getting to know the Amish I'd learned that the behavior toward wayward children differed from community to community, as well as from family to family. I was impressed with Sarah, her openness and willingness to meet her son where he was. She was a remarkably strong and wise woman.

Sarah wanted to know about my family, how many children I had and their ages. Believing Violet to be my only child, she was surprised when I told her that I had six and my oldest was sixteen.

"How old are you?" She wanted to know. Hemming and hawing, because that was not something I often divulged, I quietly responded "forty-one" hoping nobody else in the room would overhear. "Wow," she said, "I thought you were much younger than that."

You know, I really like the Amish sometimes, especially Sarah.

My day was enjoyable thus far, as was the trip home. David and I conversed, him giving me more insight into the Amish culture while Violet slept quietly in the back seat.

"David, I've seen and heard a lot today. Do you mind if I ask you a few questions to help me further understand your people and culture?"

"No." was his simple reply

Permission granted; I fired away. "How does confession work, when people commit major sin?"

"They go to the bishop, confess to him and then are, in some communities, required to publicly confess to the whole church congregation. After that all is forgiven." David added with a tone of finality.

"That seems pretty simple, almost too simple." I responded.

"Now, Haley, I don't necessarily agree with how things are done as far as that goes as a means of repentance, but it is our tradition so I go along."

"Is there ever a case where the Amish, once married, can divorce?" I asked.

"No." he simply responded.

"Not even if there is adultery, murder, or abuse of children or spouse."

"No."

"Then what happens, in a case like that?" I had to know, not understanding how that could be.

David said, "If there was child or spousal abuse the victim/s could move away, but never divorce."

"But David," I argued, "I have friends who have had to divorce because their husbands were addicted to pornography, which for them, led to other inappropriate behaviors."

Knowing how sheltered from the wickedness of the world, I needed to know "Do you know what pornography is?"

"No."

I wasn't entirely sure how to explain it to him, nor was it a comfortable thing to do however, after giving it my best shot, he seemed to understand.

"Oh," I thought to myself, "to be so innocent and not worry about exposure to pornography and all the problems that comes with it. Life really was less complicated for those simple folk."

Finally, we arrived at his house, after about seven hours traveling around. David invited me in. He and his boys wanted to see photos of the trip our families took to Colorado together a few months prior. Settling myself in the living room on the couch, I set up my laptop to show them. His boys sat right next to me watching with intensity my every move, opening the computer, typing in the password, inserting the jump drive, opening up the pictures folder. They watched my hand manipulate the mouse, wondering what it was. We went through about a hundred photos, many of which the boys were in. Prior to the trip I told David if I took them to Colorado, I got to take photos of them, to which he agreed.

Normally the Amish didn't allow their photos taken, especially of their faces. The boys LOVED looking at themselves on my computer and chose photos for me to print into a book for them. As we were doing this, I was surprised when one of the boys, with much excitement, told me they had a photo album with photos of a few of them as younger children.

"How did you get it?" I wondered aloud.

Saloma, David's wife, piped up from the kitchen, "We had a neighbor in Iowa who liked to snap photos of us from her home, where we couldn't see her doing it."

"Where you aware she was taking those photos?"

"No, we weren't." Saloma confirmed.

"Then how did you come to possess them?"

"She printed them up for us as a gift before we moved."

I chuckled, thinking to myself, 'that's just bizarre.'

Ruben, David's fourteen-year-old boy fetched the album, returning, plopping himself next to me. Opening it up for us to look at it first were pictures of their current home. "Those pictures of our home were taken by the man who drove David, baby Rosanna and I down here to look at the house before we bought it." Saloma offered.

"Why did you have pictures of the home taken?" I inquired

"So we could take them back to Wisconsin and show the other children."

"What's with the photos of all the livestock, especially their rear-ends?" I wanted to know, as we continued flipping pages, noticing most of the photo album was filled with photos of cow's hindquarters.

"Oh, we had someone take those photos to show us because we were looking at purchasing cows. We wanted to know what their udders looked like for milking." David piped in.

"Okay, weird, I'd never heard anything like that," I thought to myself, "And they saved the photos of these cow behinds, what silliness."

There were a few photos of their Iowa home with pictures of their family members; Little Harley in a wagon, Saloma in the garden, Marvin toddling around the yard. Those were the photo's that excited the children most of all.

Photos all put away Saloma extended an invitation for Violet and I to have supper with them, which we gratefully did and then we were off.

Another enjoyable day with the Amish spent. Drumming up business was not only enjoyable, but successful as well, as the calls began pouring in. I learned a lot about the Amish culture that day too, about their religious beliefs and practices, and, something that surprised me, the fact that the Amish do bend their own rules.

"No dreams come true until you wake up and go to work."
—*Amish Proverb*

One of my little passengers

19

Mad Bull

The cell phone I'd carelessly tossed on the dining room table screeched like a dying cat in the humid late May heat. On the other line was Josie Fry of Mt. Vernon asking if I could take his family to Meridian, Wisconsin the following evening leaving at 8:00 p.m. Violet was welcome to come along. The next evening while traveling down State Highway 96 in search of Josie's house, being a new driver and not terribly familiar with the community, I zoomed right by, as he stood there watching. Confused, I stopped at another Amish home to ask the man outside working in the yard the whereabouts of Josie's home. He responded by asking me to drive him the next day; which, regretfully I couldn't because I'd be in Wisconsin. He then directed me to Josie's home and, luckily, I still made it on time. He, his wife Sylvia and their four very young children joined Violet in the back seats and then I was instructed to pick up David J, Lillian and their two boys to complete the load.

As perfect as you can imagine it was how the trip went. We had perfect weather, perfect traffic and perfect alertness on my part in driving all night. The slumbering moon was still surrounded by the thick, dark, black sky, when we arrived at about 4:00 a.m. to where Josie and family would be dropped off. Violet and I continued on with David J and his family. They invited us to stay with them at Lillian's parents' home, Vernon and Mary's, a place we'd stayed before. Pulling into their long dirt drive, a large white metal shop was on our right, a garden plot on the left, bordered by the home which was really two homes attached, larger one where Lillian's parents lived, and a smaller one where her sister and brother-in-law lived. A large red barn loomed straight ahead. Violet and I stayed in the home of Lillian's younger sister Frieda. We were given an upstairs bedroom. It was clean, neat, and blue; VERY blue, it reminded me of a Smurf Village. The décor consisted of sky-blue walls, navy blue curtains, and a multiple-colored blue quilt on the bed. A simple curtained shelf, blue of course, hung on the wall which supported wedding memorabilia of glass ware, foam painted thank-you's and cards. Beside the bed, the only other furniture in the room was a beautiful Amish crafted walnut dresser covered with a dark blue cloth and green glassware, an Amish made rocking chair, and a simple wooden dining chair. That was the room. It was the perfect place for us to take a restful nap.

Violet and I were happy to nap. She, not needing as much sleep as I did due to my driving all night, woke up first, her sturdy little legs carrying her downstairs to investigate because she was hungry. Lillian gave her a cookie for breakfast; then she happily went off to play. A couple of hours later I awoke, looked out the bedroom window and saw a few Amish girls standing with Violet near a cyclone fence enclosing a chicken coop. Quickly, I dressed and went downstairs to find Violet now in the fenced off chicken area. In her pink dress, barefooted with her long curly blond hair blowing in the wind, quite a contrast to her Amish audience, she gently held a fryer in one arm while petting it with the other. The Amish girls were in awe of my little Englischer girl, watching with upturned lips and delight in their eyes. She set down her captive fryer only to boldly walk into the chicken house and pick up another one. Upon seeing me at the fence with the Amish girls, Violet thoughtfully stuck her new chicken friend's head through the fence inviting me to pet it.

It was common for Amish to use a van liberally when on a trip. Much of my day was spent driving people around while Violet remained at the Amish home playing with the children. Come dinner time (known as lunch to the city folk) I was back, and invited to dine with the family. After a tremendous dinner a few young girls began preparations for a wedding they were to attend the next day. Using the wash basin and counter in the kitchen, they unbraided their hair, washed it and re-braided it; a task normally reserved for Saturday nights in preparation for Sunday. Violet sat enthralled by this braiding ritual, thinking it beautiful, and wanted her hair braided the Amish way too; the young girls were delighted to braid my little Englischer girl's hair. To finish off the look Lillian placed a black kapp on her head; and just as fast Violet shoved it off. Quick thinking, Lillian offered Violet a red bandana instead, to which she kept on. She then pranced around showing off her new look, basking in all the attention she was granted.

Thinking Violet might want to stay inside; to keep away from all the Wisconsin mosquitos and flies, I brought Violet's pink backpack full of toys into the house and set it in the living-room for her to play with and share with the other children. The Amish children were curious and watched as Violet plopped her little body down on the floor, unzipped her backpack and pulled out her baby girl doll first. Made of plastic, skin colored, with blue eyes that opened and shut, wearing pink pajamas and a pink cap, she looked like a real baby, only smaller. Those children must never have seen such a baby doll. They were fascinated, especially by her face. Violet sweetly handed one of the admiring girls her baby, who then cradled it in her arms, looked intently at the face, and gently ran her fingers over it, caressing the eyes, ears, button nose and pursed red lips. She talked excitedly about it and running around the house showing her to others, who also took interest. She wanted that doll for herself. Dolls Amish girls were given were homemade of white cloth, stuffed, and faceless, and wearing plain Amish clothing. Violet's realistic, fancy baby was a big deal to those little girls. It warmed my heart to see my little girl so willing to share with others.

The next morning Violet and I were allowed to sleep in till 8:00 or so our time (that Amish community didn't recognize day light savings), when we were awakened by a gentle knock on the bedroom door and a "time to get up." We dressed; then went downstairs for a breakfast of warm biscuits and gravy. Violet and I sat together at the dining room table, while a few little girls, in matching blue dresses, black aprons, and black kapps stood leaning against the table staring at us as we ate. We were getting used to all the attention now so it no longer bothered us as it did in the beginning.

After breakfast it was time to drive around. "Where is the swing?" Violet wanted to know as she exited the van at David J's parents' home, where we would be spending the remainder of the day. Not having one set up, Martha, David J's mom was sweet to set one up for her on the front porch. She got to swinging right away, drawing the attention of Martha's three little granddaughters. I settled myself on the porch to watch the children play. Humming birds entertained us, flying upon the porch to suck nectar from the feeder set out for them. Wanting to capture some pictures, I pulled out my cell phone. Seeing what I was doing, the three little girls placed themselves right next to me, eyes darting from me to my cell phone with great interest. Little fingers cautiously reached out to touch the screen, I pulled back so they couldn't, but I did show them the photo's after I took them, to which they took great interest.

David summoned me to run more errands, while Violet stayed at Martha's house to play with the little girls. Upon returning I found Violet upstairs in the playroom. Computer in hand, I went upstairs to write while keeping an eye on her. No sooner had I settled down on a bench in the large open hallway next to the play room, than I had company. Two little boys practically sat themselves on my lap to get a view of my activities. They watched with great interest as my fingers flew across the keyboard making black words on the white notepad of my computer screen. Watching wasn't enough however, with a quick glance in my direction to see if I was paying attention, one little hand snuck out and touched the screen, then another the keyboard. Looking into the children's eyes, firmly, I let them know that was not okay. They didn't care. Somehow others, like a telegraph, caught wind that an interesting person was upstairs, with a fascinating device. Next thing I knew, I heard the pitter patter of little feet making their way up the enclosed staircase to the hallway where I'd settled. One by one, blue blurs with brown tops flew past me, each one with their arm reached out to touch the computer, mischievous grins on their knowing faces. Unable to type with such interruptions, I had to put the computer away and crochet instead. They were not at all interested in my crocheting, and returned downstairs.

My laptop battery was nearly out, even though I wasn't able to type much on it due to curious little children and their wayward fingers. Having no way to charge the laptop at Martha's home, I asked if there was an English house nearby with residents that would let me charge it while Violet and I napped. We walked to the neighbors about one-half mile away, as Martha said; they allowed me to charge my computer. That evening after our naps Violet and I borrowed one of the children's red wooden wagons and walked to pick the computer up. It was a beautiful afternoon, the suns brilliant rays shone brightly and the smell of fresh hay in the air. We were very much enjoying our walk home, gathering wild mustard to snack on along the way. Wanting to remember the moment, I took a picture of Violet, from a distance, in front of the Amish farm we were spending the day at. The Wisconsin landscape, rugged and rich, dairy cows dotting the open pastures, beckoned me to take a photo of it too. Violet and I worked up an appetite, so back at our van, in Martha's driveway we snacked on veggie chips. Little children, with big eyes and little hands open in longing, surrounded us, wanted us to share our snack which we happily did. My children and I eat all day, literally whereas the Amish only eat three times a day, so snacks were a welcome treat for them.

It was a beautiful night, the air cooled as dusk descended, giving way to hues of orange and deep red; silhouettes of birds flying home across the sky. Violet and I wanted a better look, so we, in our shorts, tee-shirts and sandals walked down the road stopping along the way to take photos. Blissfully strolling past a cow pasture, we hear a muuhhhrrr, rrrruuuurrrr, moo, muuhhhrrr, rrrruuuurrrr, moo getting louder and louder. Charging full speed down the hill straight toward us, with just a flimsy barbed wire fence as protection, appeared this mighty, muscular, mad bull, silver ring piercing its pink nose, giving him an even more ferocious look. He stopped right next to the fence, pawing at the dirt, snorting, with his eyes rolled back. He then stared us down, dark brown eyes narrowed, rigid, cold and hard. Gasping for air, in a panic, grabbing Violet's hand we turned around headed back to Martha's home, I then changed my mind, being too scared to pass the bull again. With much haste I drug Violet the opposite direction, toward the nearest house, which happened to be Amish. Hoping it wasn't too late, as by now, just a sliver of the glowing sun shown above the mountains, my shaky fist knocked on the door, Violet hand in mine. An elderly couple, in their pale blue night cloths, opened the door, curious looks on their faces, probably wondering why an Englischer girl and her daughter were soliciting them at that late hour. Without introduction, quivering in my voice, I quickly explained my fear of the bull. Compassionately, they told me their daughter who lived up the road had a similar experience with the animal. Still terrified, I refused to walk back by myself, especially with my daughter as visions of the bull escaping his confines ran through my head. Generously, they agreed to walk down the street with us, along with their dog Sparky for added protection. Sparky had been well trained to stay out of the road, so when they instructed Sparky to come with us, hoping he would bark at the bull and frighten it, he refused. Our temporary companions with us; we walked back toward Martha's home. Brahnk, brahnk, brahnk, a bull frog made its way across the road in front of us, though it was dark Violet spotted it, chased it to and fro as it hopped along, and finally snatched it up with her left hand. Brahnk, brahnk, brahnk...there was another one. Violet caught that one with her right hand. Brahnk, brahnk, brahnk...there was yet another one. This time Violet used both her hands to scoop up the frog. Now she had three. We'd forgotten all about the bull. He'd apparently forgotten about us and we made it safely back to Martha's house, grateful for the assistance of the elderly Amish couple. Back at the house, Violet proudly walked up to the group of Amish children standing around outside and showed them her catch. Smiles lit up their faces, arms reached out, hands extended to hold the frogs, which Violet gladly shared. Laughs of delighted children filled the air. All was well again.

Shortly thereafter it was time to go in for supper. We washed our hands, sat down at the table with the family and proceeded to eat supper buffet style. While Violet and I were still eating, the little children who'd completed their meal crawled under the dining room table to play around. Violet, who was sitting in a high chair, wearing her light up sandals, moved her feet. High pitched giggles could be heard from under the table as the Amish children noticed Violet's shoes flicker in pink and purple, lightening up the dark space under the table. That attracted even more children under the table and encouraged Violet to keep stomping her feet. What a great time everyone was having! The mothers even noticed what was going on and giggled too. The Amish children had probably never seen such a thing.

I napped a couple of times, not sleeping much, in preparation for the seven hour, four-hundred mile all night drive home. We left at 11:30 our time (10:30 slow time). We left so late because our Amish wanted to get as much family time in as possible; and who can blame them. They didn't know when they'd visit Wisconsin again.

Josie sat in front the first leg of the trip. He was quite entertaining. My GPS system, named Crazy Susie by David B, because of her directional problems, sat prominently in the center of the dash. Without asking, Josie turned the GPS to face him, and started pushing buttons. He discovered, to his delight, that there were audio books on it. He chose to play a clip from Willy Wonka and the Chocolate Factory. Tiring of that after a few minutes, he chose a book I'd never heard of. It began in ancient Egypt with a story surrounding a sarcophagus and the Catholic Church, then fast forwarded to modern times. A teen-age couple, who'd discovered the sarcophagus, had major crushes on each other, and it was quite graphic. The boy described the girl taking off her coat revealing a tight shirt forming around her breasts; crisp, hard and round like apples. Wide eyed, mouth gaping, cheeks turning red, I cast a glance Josie's way. Simultaneously, he gave me the same shocked and embarrassed look. Mortified, I quickly explained that I didn't know books were even on the GPS, let alone that one. I'd never played with the GPS audio feature before. Yet, Josie kept the book playing, which surprised me; an Amish man listening to such trash. I was uncomfortable with it, fearing what offensive language would come next. It didn't take long before a slew of cuss words and the Lord's name in vain blared out of the speaker. Josie received my shocked look again, and he finally turned the book off. Not to be discouraged, he continued searching through the audio. Gratefully, he came across classic country music, much milder and more appropriate. He let it play quite a while; again, I was surprised because I believed Amish didn't listen to music. Josie and his antics helped keep me awake through the long night drive, and for that I was obliged.

Needing a break, just south of Minneapolis we stopped. Lillian, David J's wife, empty gallon ice cream pale in hand, then took the hot seat, because, it appeared, she was car sick. It was nice to have a woman up front for a change to keep me company, and hopefully awake during the remainder of the trip home. A few minutes into the trip, Lillian bent over, reaching for the pale, quickly took the lid off and Blargh, blargh, blargh, vomited into it. I couldn't grab my peppermint essential oil fast enough to counteract the putrid odor. My nose was very sensitive. I kept essential oils in the van not only for those cases where a particular offensive odor presented itself such as when we'd pass a feed lot, or skunk, or when

112

someone in the van passed gas, but also for keeping me awake. Peppermint served both those purposes quite nicely.

"Are you alright Lillian? Can I do anything for you?" You must be quite car sick." Leaning toward me, placing her left hand on my ear, she whispered very quickly and quietly, "I am pregnant and I don't want anyone to know."

Leaning toward me, placing her left hand on my ear, she whispered very quickly and quietly, "I am pregnant and I don't want anyone to know."

Surprised, and very excited for her, as I knew she'd struggled with conceiving, leaning toward her, hand cupped near her ear, while flying down the dark, wet highway at seventy miles per hour, in disbelief, I asked her, "Does your husband know? Do your parents know?"

"Yes, they all know she assured me." Glancing back hoping no one was paying attention to our private conversation.

'Then why didn't she want me to tell anyone?' I wondered to myself.

Seeing the confusion on my face she explained, "In my culture pregnancies are kept quiet so the children are not aware until the child is born. No one is privy to that information unless they are very close family, and it isn't a topic spoken about."

I responded with a scrunched-up face, questioning in my eyes.

"I have no idea why we do it that way, it is just tradition." Lillian explained.

Enjoying the teaching moment, she was sharing with me, she volunteered, "Our women's dresses are made not just to conceal our figures, but also to expand and cover up pregnancies."

That was a new idea for me; I had to chew on for quite some time.

Things finally settled down in the van, no more offensive language; no more vomiting. Tired again, Lillian shut her eyes while I continued alone with my thoughts. We all made it home safely just as the sun rose over Missouri's rolling hills signaling the beginning of another beautiful day and the end of another memorable trip with my Amish friends.

"Unshared joy is like an unlighted candle." —*Amish Proverb*

Violet in her Amish Kapp with the chickens

20

Directionally Challenged

"I know exactly where I'm going," Vernon assured me.

"Okay," I repeated to Vernon over and over and over on what should have been a sixty mile, slightly over one hour trip to Dalton from his Blaire Community. Instead, it turned out to be a hundred-thirty mile, two-and-a-half-hour trip due to his insistence on knowing where he was going, when clearly, he had no clue.

Vernon, a red headed, squat, tough looking man of forty-four and father of eleven was the self-proclaimed navigator on that day's trip. After driving twenty-one miles back and forth through his small Amish community picking up another eight passengers; Vernon; who had the front seat, looked at me. "Haley, how would you get to Dalton from here?" he asked. Having done just that at least a few times I told him I'd take the 66 east and from there hit highway 26 south, then the 3 which led directly into Dalton. Dismissing my response, Vernon directed me to take the 205, which went southwest. We needed to go southeast.

"Okay," I responded suspiciously, in my mind believing Vernon really didn't know what he was doing. But he hired me so I did what I was told. Traveling on through Nyssa, nearing Lincoln, having gone fairly far southwest, I questioned him on it again. With disdain, he ordered me to continue on his way.

"All right" I responded with an 'I don't believe you' tone of voice, letting him know he'd been heard.

From the 205 he instructed me to take the I-73 South toward Robie Creek...still heading West. I questioned him again. "Are you sure you don't want me to get the GPS going?"

"No, I got this." Vernon snapped arrogantly, ordering me to continue on. We got within just forty-five miles of Robie Creek, still heading very much in the opposite direction of Dalton. Again, I questioned him, and again he insisted, adding a little more insight revealing his plan. "We'll find highway 3 from there." Giving him an untrusting glance, he continued justifying his logic, "That's how we always go to Dalton."

"Okay" I responded, sensing he was continuing to lead us wrong. Being very observant along the way, I noticed signs indicating we were getting closer and closer to Robie Creek. I encouraged Vernon to get out my Missouri map, which I kept in the front passenger side pocket, especially for occasions like that.

"No", he insisted. "We will see Highway 3 soon enough."

"Alright," I acknowledged with a sigh. Having driven seventy-three miles already, with no sign of Dalton, I was racking up the miles, most of them unnecessarily. Getting dangerously close to Robie Creek, Vernon relented and at my urging pulled the Missouri map out of the side pocket to find a better way. He finally decided it was time to turn around and head north.

"That's where we'll find Highway 3," he assured me.

"Okay," I happily replied, still not believing him, but grateful he'd admitted his mistake; albeit in a roundabout way; and was getting on the right track. After seven more miles of driving, we came upon the next exit.

From the back I heard men's voices in unison holler "Stop, quick! Lester, Lester!" unbeknownst to me, the van was a little too warm for one young Amish man. As quickly as possible I pulled over to the right side of the off ramp. The side door opened and out tumbled long, skinny, young Lester from the back seat, barf splattered all over his shirt and pants. A pungent smell flowed from the back of the van, and from him. He spent a few more minutes outside emptying the contents of his stomach.

Meanwhile I directed his friends to my roll of paper towel under the back bench on the left. I also offered Lester my purple spray bottle of peppermint water kept in the driver side pocket for such occasions. He cleaned up as best as he could, however, the stringy brown mucus like substance still lingered on his clothing, but at least it was dampened and smelled better. From then on Lester rode in the front with me, continually spraying himself hoping to be presentable by the time we arrived in Dalton. My stomach was weak, so I got out my peppermint oil, dabbed it under my nose, on my clothing, and in the van to help with the smell. Poor Lester; it was a long, rough ride for him.

After changing our direction to travel north on the I-73, finally, much to my amazement, we found Highway 3 as Vernon had said we would. From there we were able to get into Dalton; at last. Once in Dalton, I asked Vernon where we were going. He knew the name of the facility, but he didn't know where it was located.

"Dalton is small" he assured me, "let's just go straight down the main road and we'll be sure to find it."

Past experience from the day's journey thus far told me not to trust him. A buggy headed toward us, so I rolled down my window, waved the gentleman down and asked him where the goat milk meeting was. Good thing I did because we would have never found the venue going on Vernon's hunches. We arrived an hour late for the Organic Milk Farmers Co-op meeting, but not too late for the catered lunch they served. It was an incredible assortment of crackers, hot chili, bread, and goat cheese of all kinds.

On the way home Vernon was in the front seat with me...again. Without wasting a moment, I firmly told Vernon I would be taking them home my way. And you know what; it was only a sixty-mile drive, as I had told him. Vernon's house was the first stop. Pulling into the driveway he looked at me, and in all seriousness asked me if he had to pay the extra miles.

"Yes," I responded incredulously, "It was your fault. If those miles were my mistake, I'd pay for them." Eyes lowered in defeat? Disappointed, he relented.

A few days later, I relayed our adventurous trip to my friends Ura and Sylvia, Members of Vernon's community. Ura, animated and quick witted, boldly proclaimed, "Vernon is tighter than a frog's ass." At that Sylvia and I roared with laughter. It couldn't have been said better; many Amish were tight; tight as a frog's ass one might say.

"The best way to save face is to keep the lower half of it shut."
—*Amish Proverb*

Sign in Holmes County, Ohio

21

Thanksgiving Rush

To find a driver; having just returned from a trip to Ohio, settling into bed when I thought I heard a woman screaming and realized it was the cry of a peacock which was my phone going off. The number indicated an Amish man or woman on the other end.

"Hello" I answered. The stuttering older sounding voice of a man responded, "Hi, this is Harley Zook of Blaire. Can you take our family to Centerville, Missouri Wednesday evening the twenty-third? We want you to bring the scholars (school aged children) home early Friday morning so they can attend their classes. The adults will remain to spend Thanksgiving with family."

"I'd be happy to; however, I'm already taking a load up to Wisconsin over Thanksgiving, leaving early Wednesday morning, returning Friday sometime. If it gets down to the wire and you can't find anyone else, I could take your family up Tuesday evening, and pick them up on Saturday."

Harley, a little bit of shock in his voice returned, "Oh, no, no, no, that won't do. The children can't miss any school; they must stay till Wednesday and be back Friday morning to attend their classes."

"Wow" I thought to myself, 'the children have school on Friday and can't miss any classes, even to travel with family; pretty strict.' So, I tried to convince Harley otherwise, that his children could miss a couple of days of school. He insisted, "No, the Amish have to be in their classes."

"Okay" I resigned, "I wish you the best of luck in finding a ride for Thanksgiving."

Two weeks later while enjoying a rare day at home, after six straight days of travel, while at an auction with my youngest boys the phone rang. Looking at the number I knew it was from the Amish. Out of breath, tired, and cold because I'd just returned from a trip, hadn't eaten yet that day, and further exhausted myself by riding my bike to the Auction, I near breathlessly answered the phone with a weak, "Hello". The man's voice, deep and in a rush of stuttering words inquired, "Hi, this is Harley Zook, do you have plans for today?"

Sighing, because I really wanted to spend the day with my family, I forced myself to cheerfully respond, "No, how can I help you?"

Unabashedly, stating what he sensed in my response, he queried, "Now, did I detect a sigh in your response?"

Quickly, with emphasis, "no, no" I assured him, perhaps trying to convince myself as well.

He continued "My wife has been thinking on how we can get to Centerville and have the children still attend their classes; she's always coming up with ideas. We'd like you to drive us to Centerville, this afternoon then on Monday morning drive our scholars back home in time for their classes at 9:30 a.m. The rest of us will stay the week and get another ride home. Can you do that for us?" He asked, hopefulness being forced into his voice, trying to cast aside all doubt.

"Yes, I'd be happy to" I responded. "What time would you like me to pick you up?"

"Oh 3:30 or 4:00 this afternoon."

"Okay, I will be there at 3:30 this afternoon then."

Grateful he wasn't in a terrible rush; I'd be able to be with my boys at the auction a bit longer. "Harley, how do I get to your home?"

"Harley, how do I get to your home?"

"You were there last week, don't you remember?"

"No, please, direct me to your home." He was correct, I was there recently; driving twenty-one miles through the community where houses, streets and people all looked the same, which made it hard for me to remember where I'd been and whom I'd seen. He gave me the directions then asked if I had a cargo box. His family would fill up my van and they wanted to pack food so their family members, where they would be guests, wouldn't have to rely on their hosts to feed the all of them, which amounted to thirteen people.

"There is an available cargo box stored at the community's milk house; if you and a son will come and load it on the van we can use it."

"Great, see you soon" said a happy Levi getting his last-minute wish to go to Centerville. I returned to the auction and treasuring the few remaining hours with my children before another trip.

My family was surprised that I was leaving yet again. Sunday, I hauled to the local hospital, from Monday to Wednesday I was in Indiana, Thursday I hauled a van of eleven men to a raw milk convention in Iowa, and Friday I hauled a couple of people to run errands in town. Surely my Saturday would be free we all thought. Part of me wished I had refused so that I could spend the day with my own children.

After the auction and securing a few toys for my children for Christmas, I rode my bike home to get the truck, drive to the auction, load my purchases up, return home then pack for a two-day trip to Centerville, Missouri. Violet was invited to come along with me; however, she opted to stay at home and attend meetings with her daddy. Saddened, having never traveled overnight with the Amish without her, it was her choice.

Assured of the wellbeing of my family, at 3:00 I left my home to pick up the Zook family. I arrived ten minutes early, at 3:20, pulled into the drive, stopped next to the walkway leading up to the side door of the house, left the van running and waited. Shortly thereafter, a middle aged, average size man with a graying beard, and noticeably crooked yellow teeth came out to inform me that no one was ready to go.

"My wife didn't expect to be going to Centerville today so she's not quite got the whole family packed yet. I have to finish getting ready too. When I'm done, we can go get the cargo box."

"Okay," I said, happy to wait and get some crocheting done. About fifteen minutes later Harley showed up, jumped in my van and directed me where to go to fetch his fifteen-year-old son Marvin who would help him load the box on the van. Pulling into the farm, where he worked full time as a farm hand, Harley warned me that Marvin was terribly prone to car sickness. Getting in the van, I offered him use of my digestive oil, and Harley gave him a ginger pill, and then offered Marvin the front seat for the duration of our travels. After fetching the box, we returned to Harley's home to gather the rest of his family, who still weren't ready. I drank a lot of water, and by that time, needed to use the outhouse. When I asked Harley, he looked at me wide eyed, and responded, "All we have is the outhouse, are you okay using that?" Apparently, he didn't notice that I had just asked to use the outhouse, and was unaware of how many outhouses I'd used in the past few months. Finally understanding, he directed me and off I went. Walking through the wash house, and opening the door that led into the outhouse, my nose was filled with the particularly unpleasant smell of weeks old stool and urine that had piled up in the primitive facility. To the left above my head was a small rectangle shape opening to the outside for allowing in fresh air. Directly opposite the opening was a shelf holding an air freshener spray can. It was a two holer, two empty toilet paper holders, one on either side of the small room, were the only other things on the plywood wall. Down, to my right was a box full of sheets of newspaper on the outhouse's dirt floor. That was to be used as a toilet paper; not a terribly comfortable thing to clean oneself with, which I found distasteful, but it was better than a corn cob or nothing at all. Not to mention what I had to sit on; a crudely cut worn particle board, oval shaped hole, with a five-gallon bucket below to catch my excretions. Yikes! I was glad to have my essential oil water-based spray sanitizer with me to spray down surfaces and myself when done.

We finally left for Centerville at about 5:15 p.m.; the sky had darkened by then. The deer were out for their evening snacks; it was a miracle we didn't hit any along the way. Everyone in the Zook family was very excited to be traveling, as due to financial constraints, it was a rare treat for them. Harley sat in the bench behind me so Marvin could have the front seat. When not tending to his family, that man talked my ear off as very few Amish men had before. His favorite topic was religion. He asked me questions about my religion, and openly volunteered information about his, I was fascinated listening to him and learned much about the Amish faith. Before we left, I gathered music, mostly hymns, and Christmas music, hoping they might be open to listening to it on the trip, especially it being the Christmas season. The topic of music was brought up. Harley informed me, that due to his community's standard in regards to music only live human singing voices were allowed to be listened to, no radio, no concerts, no instruments of any kind, not even the mouth harp (harmonica) were to be heard by their ears if at all possible. Of course, there were allowances when out in public, if music was playing it couldn't be helped. However, they were not to intentionally listen to anything other than live voices singing, as far as music went. Not entirely understanding, as I'd never heard of anyone having such standards, I asked him, "Harley, what is the logic behind no instruments owned or listened to, and only listening to live singing voices?"

He responded in the typical manner I'd found to be common among the Amish when I asked questions about their culture, "It's just the way I was just brought up I guess."

"What harm does playing or listening to an instrument do?" I asked, not satisfied with his route answer; sincerely wanting to understand.

"Well, let me think for a minute... I can explain it in my language, but how to explain it in yours...?" "Humph," he continued, "I've heard music played on the radio where artists took gospel hymns and put them to country music. Now for me, country music doesn't bring me closer to God, while the sounds of it cause me to think different thoughts that might lead me in a direction away from God. Do you get what I'm saying?"

"Hmmm, so the way the music is played invites your thoughts to turn from God, the music doesn't honor God, yet the words might, which due to the music, despite the words, can lead one from God?" I questioned.

"Yes, something like that" he confirmed.

"I can see how that would be," I acknowledged, adding for clarification, "In addition, there is music that I feel brings me closer to God, songs and instruments that warm my heart and invite God's spirit."

"Well," he said, understanding, "that's just a line I don't want to cross, it is best if we just don't listen to any music at all, if we do, we will desire it more and it can lead us down a dangerous path."

"Okay, I can see how you can come to that conclusion." I conceded.

That was an enlightening conversation; I hoped for the both of us.

Turning his attention back to his family, young Marvin almost made the whole trip without throwing up; just a few miles out of Centerville, sadly, he lost it.

Levi's family didn't know they were coming. That was another behavior typical of the Amish culture in some communities, they would travel long distances to arrive at a family or friends' home, expecting room and board at all hours of the day completely unannounced. From my cultural background such behavior would be seen as rude. If twelve people would be visiting, I would want to make sure I was at home, would have time to spend with them, that the house was clean, that there would be enough room for everyone to stay, and that I would have enough food to feed the large group. Not with the Amish, as it was just part of their culture. They always seemed to be ready for guests.

Harley directed me to stop at his brother's home where he invited himself and his large family to stay. With everyone having found lodging, Sarah, Harley's oldest child stayed in the van and directed me to her relative's house nearby where she would ask if she and I could stay. Just before we arrived at Marvin and Martha's they drifted off to sleep. It was 9:30 p.m. and the van pulling into the drive awoke them, so Marvin, with his flashlight, and Martha got up to check things out. They invited us in to sit by the woodstove, which was still warm, while they readied beds for us. Typically, the Amish only heated the main floor of their homes, so the upstairs, which was shut off by a door, was cold.

I was grateful for kind people, safe travels, and to be going to bed; however, it was a cold, restless night's sleep.

I stayed in Centerville all day Sunday attending my own church services and otherwise keeping to myself. At 4:00 a.m. Monday morning I drove to Harley's brother's house to pick up his scholars and deliver them to their school before class started at 9:30 a.m. Before leaving, while waiting for the children to get ready at Harley's brothers, Harley and I chatted. It surprised me that he would allow me, a near total stranger to be alone traveling with his precious children so far. Harley, smiling, looking straight into my eyes, in all seriousness, told me he was, in his own way, 'doing a background check' on me while traveling to Centerville. He did that by observing my mannerisms and asking questions, as well as by sharing his beliefs to see how I responded, and if I would be respectful of them. Apparently, the test was passed, because he felt comfortable having me around his children. Breathing a sigh of relief, I wanted the Amish to trust me; I took my job very seriously. Along the way the children mostly slept, while we traveled in silence, thoughts occupying my mind. The trip went smoothly; the children were complete angels. How glad I was to get to know the Zook family and help them work out their last-minute Thanksgiving plans. Not only was I a driver, I was also a friend.

"If you always wait for the right time, you might never begin."
—*Amish Proverb*

Turkey ready for butchering

22

Doggonit!

Clippity-clop, clippity-clop, clippity-clop, stepping off the treadmill, I took a couple of deep breaths, shook out my arms, and picked up the phone trying to conceal my labored breathing. "Hello." The child like soft voice on the other end responded, "Hi Haley. This is Lester. Can you come run me into town and be at my house this morning by 9:30?" It was 9:15. I lived twenty minutes' drive from the man and was drenched in sweat. "Let me throw some clean clothes on and I'll come as fast as possible," I assured him.

Workout cut short, I left pulling into his driveway about 9:45. His long, thin legs hastily carried him from the house to my van's front passenger door, which he opened. Sticking his head in, he asked if I minded if his dog rode along. Having never had a dog in my van and wanting to keep it that way, my first inclination was to say, "No!" Indicating for him to look into my van and notice how dirty it was; evidence of children's food, mud and toys, throughout, I relented. "Yeah, it's okay if a dog rides in the van." Lester pointed behind him to the right, about fifty feet off to a fenced-in kennel where a large black and brown German Shepard named Lassie was kept. Upon seeing what I had just acquiesced to; second thoughts flooded my mind. "Was she going to be friendly? Dangerous? Mean? Was she going to destroy my van?" At my approval, Lester went into the basement, returning with a leash and a blanket. He fetched Lassie, opened the back doors of my van, laid the blanket down and had Lassie hop up into the cargo area behind the back most bench. I was nervous about having such a large, strong dog in my van, but Lassie behaved well.

Lester went back into the house returning with his tow-headed, green eyed, three-year-old boy Andy who would ride along with us. I wondered what he would come up with next to bring along, a horse or a chicken.

He climbed into the seat next to me holding his toddler in his arms. "We are taking the dog to the vet for her rabies shot," Lester informed me, "But let's first go to the chiropractor." After the chiropractor Lester had me take him to the bank, Wal-Mart, Orscheln's and, at last, to the vet. Lassie stayed in the vehicle the whole time, perfectly behaved, smiling and wagging her tail.

Errands done in town, we returned to the Amish community to make stops at the bulk foods store, The Bent 'N Dent, then two different Amish homes before finally taking Lester, his dog Lassie, and his little boy Andy home. For three- and one-half hours of driving around town including wait time, not to mention wear and tear on my van and fuel costs, I was paid just twenty-five dollars. Those were the breaks. The expectation among the drivers was that they take the very small, low paying jobs in order to be hired for the long distance, high paying ones. There were other benefits as well. One could learn a lot by asking well thought out questions and listening to their answers. That was the case for me that morning.

While traveling along and visiting, I asked Lester if he'd been to Ohio before. I was going to be taking him, his wife and baby girl (Andy would be staying in the community with family), and eight other community members there leaving that very evening. "Yeah," Lester responded. "I went to Ohio a couple of years ago when I was living in Wisconsin."

Curious, I asked, "Oh, what for?"

Lester answered, "Well, I went to have a balloon treatment." Immediately visions of a bright red balloon came to mind. I asked with as much seriousness as I could muster, "What is a balloon treatment?"

Matter of factly, he told me. "Well, it's where a doctor inserts a balloon in your nose and blows it up."

Dying to understand more and constraining myself from bursting out laughing, I pried, "And, what is that supposed to do for you?"

"Well, I went because I was having major back problems and it was supposed to help me with my back pain."

"Did it?"

Emphatically, Lester said, "Yes, it helped better than anything I ever tried before."

"Did it hurt?"

"No" he returned assuredly.

"Did they knock you out for the procedure?"

"Nope, I was fully awake."

I had to know where that young Amish man came up with such a treatment method. "Where did you hear about the doctor?"

"Oh," He replied. "It was in the Amish newspaper, Plain Interests."

"Hmmm, I've read several Plain Interests papers over the course of my travels with you all,"

"Yeah," he acknowledged. "I was thinking I might need to stop by and see the balloon doctor when we are in Ohio this week. My back is acting up. Though to really get the full effects of the treatment, I would need to stay for a few days to receive treatment each day and then return every couple of months. I don't know if that would be possible."

"Yeah, that is a predicament" I concurred.

I thought to myself, "How could someone have a balloon blown up their nose as a way of healing. It just sounded like a crock, not to mention uncomfortable. Where do they come up with these ideas?" I was glad it worked for him, glad we had options, and glad to drive Lester to town that cold winter morning. Even though I only made $25.00 and had a smelly, slobbery, hairy dog in my van, it was worth it.

"Each day comes bearing its gifts, so untie the ribbons."
—*Amish Proverb*

Lassie the dog

23

Surprise Visitor

At home, fuzzy cotton-candy blue blanket over my legs, fingers typing speedily away on the laptop computer, my phone rang. Hating to have my morning studies interrupted, I answered anyway. "Hello?"

"Hi. My name is Phillip Schrock from Mosier, Illinois," the quiet, deep, muffled, older sounding voice responded. Having a hard time making out what he said, I politely asked him to repeat himself.

He did, and then continued, "Do you know if Atlee Byler will be in town this weekend? He'll be getting some visitors."

"I have no idea," I responded.

"Well, if he is, will you please let him know company will arrive on Saturday morning? Don't tell him who it is."

Confused, because I'd never received such a call and could hardly understand the man on the other end of the line two hundred fifty miles away, I asked for clarification. "Is it you that will be coming?"

"Yes, but don't tell him please. Just let him know that somebody is coming and if he won't be there will you please call and leave a message at 618-665-1706 letting me know."

"Of course, I'm happy to. Is there anything else I can do for you Phillip?"

"No, that does it. Thank you!"

"I'm happy to help."

Confused at what had just happened, I immediately called a friend who was with his Amish work crew from the same community as Atlee Byler. I had no idea who Phillip was, how he knew who I was, or how he got my phone number. After hearing my story, Vernon, the work crew boss, explained that Phillip's call was perfectly normal in his world. That was how the Amish found out if friends and loved ones would be home so they could show up unexpectedly for a visit and be assured those they were seeking would be there. It seemed ill mannered to me that company would show up without advance notice.

The next day an Illinois number appeared on my phone.

"It must be Phillip" I thought to myself. It was. He was checking to see if I did what he'd asked. I had, and yes indeed, Atlee would be home I informed him.

While I was shopping at the Amish Bent 'N Dent store just a mile from his home that Saturday morning, I received a call from Atlee. "Hey Haley, who was coming to my house? They haven't arrived yet. Are they still coming?"

"Atlee, you know I can't tell you who is coming. I was sworn to secrecy. And you, the bishop, asking me to rat on someone?" I teased.

"Okay, okay" he relented. "Where are they coming from?"

"Again, Bishop, I can't tell you. I was sworn to secrecy. You, an ecclesiastical leader, wouldn't want me to break my promise, would you?"

"No, I guess not" he replied in frustration not appreciating my teasing.

I enjoyed having the upper hand on the bishop. Because I would not tell him what he wanted to know, he gave up and I assumed went on with his day as normal.

That Saturday morning the roads were covered in ice and no sane person would have driven on them, but there I was driving around the Amish community. That afternoon, Phillip made it safely to Mt. Vernon. The purpose of his trip, I later learned, was to investigate the idea of moving to the Mt. Vernon community with his two sisters. He surprised Atlee by dropping that on him. I thought to myself he must have done it that way because the community couldn't refuse him; surprise was his weapon of choice. How's that to spring on someone unannounced? Would anyone really do this? Not in my world!!

Aftermath: It was a warm, sunny, breezy late summer day in Carlton, a lovely small town on the Mississippi river in the north east corner of Missouri. I'd just left the Amish wedding noon meal to wait at the library and work on my book when my phone rang.

Atlee Byler's deep voice had an air of uncertainty as he bravely queried me. "Hi Haley, I have a question for you."

As a driver, I'd driven Atlee a few times; however, I knew his call wasn't in regards to wanting a ride. "Okay, what can I help you with Atlee?" I asked him knowing the answer already.

"How do you like your property in Eagle Crest?" he asked, discomfort obvious in his voice.

"I like it very much."

"Would you be willing to sell it?" He brazenly asked.

"No. I'm keeping it. Is this in regards to the visit from Phillip earlier this year? Are you asking about my property on his behalf?" I wondered if he'd noticed all the work that had been going on at the property, all the vehicles and equipment I'd recently moved there, including an RV I stayed in a couple of times a week, not to mention the bulldozing going on in preparation to build a house.

"Yes, I am."

"Well, I just have a tiny plot of land compared with many of you in the community...David B, Josie, Vernon, Otto, and you. I might suggest one of you sell him a small piece of your abundant land."

At that statement he responded with silence, probably shocked that I, a woman, would speak so frankly to him, the community's bishop. Perhaps the Amish felt entitled to my land. It was in their community, and I purchased it from David B, about a year and a half ago. David was quite anxious to rid himself of it when I purchased it. With an uncomfortable, "well, thank you, goodbye" that was the end of our awkward conversation. I supposed I'd hear from them again. A couple of months ago, while driving David B to Wisconsin, he asked me to sell the property to an Amish family as well. He got the same response from me. I wished Phillip luck, but I was keeping my little piece of heaven in Amish country.

"If you can't have the best of everything, make the best of everything you have." —*Amish Proverb*

Traveling through town after shopping

24

Trailer Troubles

During my tenure as an Amish driver, I'd resigned myself to unexpectedly being awakened by their summons early in the morning. Most of them were farmers after all, and believed the rest of us to be on their same crazy schedule. It was no different that Tuesday morning in early March. Screech, shriek, scream sang my tortured cat sounding peacock phone ring. A Blaire number appeared on my call screen which wasn't in my contacts. I figured it was the Amish. "Hello," I answered. From the other end a man responded, "Hi, this is Menno Fry. Do you have a six-passenger truck and a trailer?"

"Yes. I have a medium size six-passenger truck and a small trailer," I responded for clarification.

"Great!" he said. "How big is your trailer?"

"It's six to eight feet wide and eight to ten feet long," I answered, not knowing for sure myself. I didn't pay attention to such things, and hadn't ever owned or pulled a trailer till I started hauling the Amish. "Okay. I've tried all the other drivers but they were unavailable so you ought to work for this. I should be able to take apart what needs hauled, a water tank and some other equipment. Can you be at my house tomorrow morning at 7:00 a.m.?" He requested.

Now, it'd been suggested to me by other drivers that when the Amish call don't ask a lot of questions, just take what they say, do your best and go on. That is what I did, trusted the man and didn't ask a lot of questions. I informed him of the details on my truck and trailer and figured he knew what he was doing. That was the first time Menno had called me, however, I'd driven his son, Roy, a few times and liked and trusted him.

The next morning, I showed-up in my pickup truck with my trailer. Coming out to greet me, sizing things up, was Menno. He was middle aged, of very slight build, with numerous deep wrinkles around his eyes, and black, thinning, short hair not common for an Amish man.

"Oh, this is your trailer. Well, that might be too small," he reasoned out loud.

"Okay. I've got some other drivers' numbers in my phone. Why don't I call and see about finding a bigger one before we head out," I offered.

Unable to locate a bigger trailer, Menno conceded, "Well we will go with what we have and work with it."

He and his son Irvine got in my truck and we went to pick up his other sons Roy, Jake and Larry. Fully loaded with me and two men on the front bench and three men on the back bench, we set off for Cottage Grove, Missouri, not far from Robie Creek. I'd never been there before so I wasn't familiar with the route.

Upon arriving at the goat milk cheese factory in Cottage Grove, the boys immediately got to work moving the property owner's large milk tank. The tank would not fit into my trailer, or my canopied truck bed. The business owner, Heather, had a pickup truck, so she hauled the milk tank to the other facility while we followed her. Milk tank delivered, we returned to the original location, but not before swapping out my small trailer for the eighteen-foot flatbed parked at the second facility.

My truck was medium sized and just one-half ton. Never having pulled such a long trailer before, I was concerned if I or my truck could handle it. Backing up to a loading dock, I waited and read a book while the men worked loading the trailer. Glancing back periodically, I watched those five short, wisps of men all wearing dark grey denims, thick dark blue handmade coats and straw hats, load a long thin blue metal sawmill belt into the trailer.

The steel object did not come apart as Menno thought it might. They got it on to the eighteen-foot trailer, though it didn't fit. It hung off another six feet. How could Menno even remotely believe that it would have fit in my trailer I wondered? Luckily, I had straps they were able to use to attach the object firmly to the trailer. Loaded, I said a little prayer asking that we would have safe travels.

The men joined me in the truck and we were off.

Being near a big city with the Amish one could expect to make a lot of unplanned stops. There I was in my truck towing an eighteen-foot trailer, with equipment hanging off the end, having never driven anything like that before and they wanted me to take them shopping in the big city. Heavy traffic, narrow lanes, pedestrians, and tight parking spots were my obstacles. Not to mention that I was in near panic mode because the trailer was too long and too heavy for my small truck to pull. The load wasn't properly placed, and part of it hung off the back causing the trailer and my truck to swerve as we traveled down the congested roads. Hands tightly gripping the steering wheel and eyes darting to and fro, I was not thrilled but took it in stride as a learning experience to develop more skills.

We stopped at Menards first. Larry, a young father, went into Menards returning with two large wooden doors. He set those on the left side of the trailer next to the saw mill equipment. He did not strap the doors down, nor were there rails or walls on the trailer to confine them. I was nervous that doors would fly off the back and cause an accident. Remember, I was a city girl used to thinking in city ways and being very careful about everything. They were country boys who had a vastly different paradigm and knew things I didn't. I made a conscious decision to trust. It worked out. The doors stayed put. I'm sure the men were amused at my obvious worrying though.

Next stop was the Stockyards to look at walnut wood. There I had to back the trailer straight up against a fence to park it. Luckily, long trailers were fairly easy to backup and were definitely easier to control than short trailers so, I managed okay, for a city girl.

Four of the five men left to look at the walnut while I sat in the truck crocheting; Menno remained directly behind me as my companion.

Some Amish men were reserved, while others were awfully nosy. Menno, whom I'd never driven before, was the nosy type. While minding my own business up front, his gravelly voice remarked, "Hey Haley, so I hear you're going through a divorce right now. You know all you need to do is forgive."

In utter disbelief at what I'd just heard, my hands stopped manipulating the crochet needle. I stared down thinking for just a moment on how to respond. My personal life was none of that man's business and I had no idea how the Blaire Amish knew, as I'd told no one there. Looking up, turning around, and surveying Menno with a questioning expression, I inquired, "Where did you learn about that?"

Returning my questioning with a smile, as if it were obvious, he replied, "The Amish Telegraph."

Oh, my stars! I thought to myself. His brazen, bold statement surprised and offended me. My personal life was mine, not for gossip. After all, I was only a driver. I wondered then, did that make me part of their community? If so, that was not a community of which I wanted to be a part. I was aware that everyone gossiped, but I didn't expect it from that seemingly godly man and minister in his community.

"Okay," I muttered, hoping to put the matter to rest. I returned to crocheting fingerless gloves for my eleven-year-old boy, as if the comment had never been made.

Yet Menno continued from the back, "You know Haley, my wife and I have been married for thirty-seven years and we still love one another. We just have to forgive."

Obviously, Menno was not going to drop the subject. Placing yarn and needle back in my purse, propping myself up against the driver side door and turning my head to the right looking back at him, I commented, "You know Menno, it takes two people to make and break a marriage. I understand the principle of forgiveness. I have been reading and studying up on the atonement and this event has given me the opportunity to gain a deeper understanding of that principle."

To which Menno responded by looking at me cross-eyed and tilting his head to the left as if he had no idea what I had just said.

"Menno, you do know what the atonement means don't you, as a Christian, Bible reading man?"

"Well, I read my Bible in German so, no, I'm not familiar with that word."

Understanding the word is different in his language, I explained "The atonement refers to the process Jesus Christ went through in the Garden of Gethsemane suffering for our sins and His subsequent death and resurrection that we may be washed free of our sins and return to Him."

Menno still had a puzzled look on his face while nodding as if he understood. Abruptly he changed the subject.

"Haley, so I hear that you're a Mormon*," he boldly stated.

My eyes widened and my mouth dropped open as I looked at Menno and demanded, "Menno, where did you hear about that? You don't even know me." He lifted his head up and with an expression of surprise replied, "The Amish telegraph of course."

My stars, I thought. How interesting could I possibly be? Have they nothing else to talk about?"

"So, Menno," I persisted. "You do know David Brady, right? He's been the milkman in the community for years."

"Yes, I Know David Brady fairly well."

"Okay," I continued, "Did you know that David Brady is a Mormon?"

Introspective, he paused and then answered, "No, I did not know David Brady was a Mormon."

Sighing in disbelief I continued, "Menno, do you know who Keith and Ruth Brady are?"

"Yes, I know them."

"Menno, I know for a fact they have driven for your community since it began seventeen years ago and they are very well-known, well-liked drivers."

"Yes," agreed Menno

"Did you know that Keith and Ruth Brady are Mormons?"

Menno's eyes shifted as he paused, obviously thinking. Finally, he responded with a drawn-out "Nooo, I did not know that they were Mormon."

That surprised me, but I took him at his word.

What to make of the situation? I wondered. Thank goodness at that point the four other men returned. Who knew what other surprises Menno may have had for me had we continued our conversation.

After several hours, we finally returned to Blaire. The men unhooked Heather's trailer from my truck and informed me that Heather was to pay for the trip. I was to collect payment from her upon returning her trailer. The trailers would be exchanged on Friday at which point payment would be collected. Not entirely believing the men about Heather paying for the trip, I called to confirm with her. Indeed, she had agreed to pay because the boys did some work for her.

I decided to call a very experienced driver, Steven, whose main job was to haul equipment and livestock for the Amish, to ask him how to charge for the swapping of trailers. The men hired the use of my trailer believing it would work, and it didn't. It was their mistake. I had to drive another five hours, pay for fuel, and cause wear-and-tear on my vehicle to remedy the situation. Steven suggested I should charge, but maybe discount it by $0.25 a mile because I wouldn't be hauling equipment. I knew there would be some resistance to my perfectly reasonable request of being compensated for the trailer swap.

That Friday, my two youngest children and I pulled into Menno's drive. There were several buggies, obviously visitors. It was noon time, so I suspected he had guests for supper. Menno, his thin black hair blowing in the wind, wore black suspenders, a light blue shirt and black boots. He walked up to the truck and greeted me, "Oh good! You're here to return the trailer."

"Yes, I'm here to return the trailer and Heather is willing to pay for Wednesday's trip, however, because of this miss-judgment on your part and my having to drive to Cottage Grove again and all the time and expense involved I am going to have to charge you," I explained.

Shaking his head, Menno's disposition changed. From the expression on his face, I realized he thought I was trying to take advantage. "Menno, I would like $150 to swap back the trailers please." I politely requested.

Then, the interrogation began. "Well, how many miles did we accumulate on Wednesday?"

"Two-hundred and fifty," I responded. "Remember all the running around we did? Jennifer is paying for your trip down there plus all the running around," I added trying to stay strong in my argument.

"How much were you charging me a mile?"

"The agreed upon price of $1.15. I'm only charging you $0.95 a mile to return the trailer," I explained hoping to soften the blow.

He simply did not want to pay, but he did, then he helped me load the trailer onto the truck and I went on.

Steven warned me that the Amish would respond that way, that was how they always responded. He advised me to just deal with it and not worry. Steven experienced many situations where the Amish were upset with him but they always called him back, and they always got over it, so I knew that what I did was within reason. Staying strong I realized was my only option, and that he would call me again; I wasn't really sure that I wanted him to though.

After that experience, I learned to press for details to avoid such situations.

Relieved to be done with that troublesome experience, the children and I were free. We drove to Cottage Grove to return the trailer, and then we did like the Amish and visited the big city.

"Advice is like cooking. You should try it before you feed it to others." — *Amish Proverb*

*Mormons – Officially known as members of The Church of Jesus Christ of Latter-Day Saints

The load on a borrowed trailer

25

Samuel Shetler from Helena, Missouri

The Amish people never ceased to interest me. Being in the taxi driving business as I was afforded me the opportunity to get to know all kinds of folks. It was through Toby D in Blaire and Toby Otto in Mt. Vernon, that I met my most memorable passenger thus far. I couldn't imagine anyone taking that title from him either.

Toby D had hired me to drive a load of Amish to Centerville, Missouri. At the same time, I was to tow a trailer carrying a machine to be delivered for repair. The day prior to our trip I dropped my flatbed trailer off at Toby's house so he could load it up and be ready to go the next morning. Pulling into Toby's drive the next day, I was greeted by his young adult son Freeman who directed me as to where to place the trailer. Observing our going-ons from the other side of the yard was Samuel Shetler, a pale, thin man in his mid-sixties. Distinctive and slightly hunched over, he unabashedly strode to my van, leaned in very closely through my open window and introduced himself.

"Hi, my name is Samuel Shetler from Helena, Missouri. My wife died in June," he unabashedly stated. "Since October, I've visited forty-three different Amish communities," he added with an air of exuberance.

Small notebook and pen in his thin wrinkled hands, he asked me, "You're a driver huh? Can I have your name and phone number? I like to keep track of who I meet. I just might need a driver sometime."

Taken aback at such bold behavior and curious as to his intentions, I looked across the lane at Freeman for some clue as to how to respond to that peculiar man. Freeman shrugged his shoulders and shook his head expressing to me his confusion and embarrassment for Samuel's bizarre behavior. Not sure how to respond other than with my name and phone number, that's what I gave him. I felt uncomfortable giving him my number, yet I figured it was possible he would share it with others with whom it would be a pleasure for me to drive.

Having my name and number recorded, just as fast as he came, he left with a, "Thank you, Haley. Good to meet you."

"Good to meet you too Samuel," I responded, not sure that it really was. I took him to be a little crazy. I wondered why he'd traveled so much. Was he mourning his wife's death or celebrating it and looking for a new one? The answer would come later.

I never expected to see or hear from Samuel again. A friend of mine, the milk man in Blaire, had the pleasure of transporting Samuel from the Blaire community to the neighboring community that I frequently drove for, Mt. Vernon.

■ ■ ■

Math had always been a weak subject for me, whether it was with numbers or situations. Tuesday morning I'd just returned from my trip to Centerville with Tony D and family. Having driven home all night, my bed

156

never looked as good as when I crawled into it at 8:00 that morning. At 8:15 my phone rang; so much for sleeping. It was Toby Otto in Mt. Vernon. He spoke quietly, quickly and was very vague, which wasn't at all helpful to me in my exhausted state. What I gathered was that he wanted to know of my availability that afternoon, around two or three o'clock, to run a man around, and possibly into Iowa. He didn't tell me who the man was, nor did it occur to me to ask. I agreed to the job, always up for an adventure and not caring who it could be. I just desperately wanted to go back to sleep. Not knowing what was in store, my head immediately hit the pillow and dreamland began.

Forcing alertness after only a few hours of fitful sleep, I pulled into Toby's driveway where he was relocating his buggy next to the chicken coop. He stopped, waved to me and proceeded on. Hearing my minivan pull into the drive, Samuel Shetler from Helena, Missouri appeared from the basement door immediately recognizing me. Oh no, I thought, what have I gotten myself into? Zestfully, he greeted me with a large smile and a dramatic flick of the round, walnut size growth on the lower left side of his neck. "Remember me," he asked?

How could I forget? I thought to myself. I'd never seen a man behave that way. Before he'd made such a dramatic display of the growth on his neck, I didn't notice it. Trying to keep from revealing my true feelings, I managed to offer a polite, and hopefully pleasant, "Hi Samuel, glad to see you again." Though I wasn't sure I was. Apparently, Tony was thinking of sending me off with Samuel alone. Gasp! What a great relief it was that he volunteered to go along with us, wherever it was, and none of us quite knew. An adventure for sure, it was going to be.

■ ■ ■

Thankfully, Tony was in the front seat with me, and the enthusiastic, rearing to go Samuel in the seat behind him. We were ready to go wherever Samuel decided. At his request, first we went to Levi P's home about one-half mile away. Samuel wanted to see if he could purchase a cream separator from Levi, as Samuel was apparently in the business of selling cream separators. And, according to him, quite a few people wanted to purchase them. I had no idea what a cream separator was. I wanted to ask him, but knew better than to do that because he already talked too much. Levi wasn't home, so we continued down the highway. About a quarter of a mile farther, a large truck filled with Amish passed us. Samuel took notice and thought Levi P might be among the passengers so we turned around and returned to Levi's house. Sure enough, Levi P was in the truck. No sooner had I stopped the van than Samuel leaped out to accost Levi before he was even aware that we were there.

While Levi and Samuel were discussing business, a slight, aged man appeared on the side deck of Levi's house. His name was Abe Miller and he ended up taking Toby's post in the front seat of my van. I'd never met Abe before. Apparently, he needed to get out of the house as he spent most of his days at home. Samuel; sad because he couldn't obtain any cream separators since Levi was in the welding business, not kitchen appliance sales; returned to my van. He, along with a silent, blank faced Abe, and a confused Toby who hopped in behind me, now sat behind Abe. We were off... to a location that was anyone's guess.

I headed toward town and expected to get instruction from there. Interrupting my internal reflection on the past day's events was an energetic Samuel, "Haley, you see, I lost my large intestine years ago and have this sack hanging out of my torso area that acts as my large intestine now. Due to this condition, I must take no-doze as it helps with my digestion. I'm out of NoDoz and wonder where a pharmacy is."

"I have no idea," I informed him, not one to take medications myself, over the counter or otherwise.

"We could try the Hy-Vee," suggested Toby.

"Yes, yes," responded Samuel. So, to the Hy-Vee it was; our second stop.

I found a parking spot near the front doors and let the three men go into the store, while I was content to stay in the van and crochet while, if possible, processing what was going on. Moments later an excited Samuel returned, with his two companions, proclaiming he was able to purchase the desired no-doze pills.

Hmmm, where will we go next, I wondered? Just then, Samuel, not leaving anything to the imagination, piped up "I need to go see Benny Zook in Woodburn, I want him to check my blood again. Last time I was there he found parasites in my blood that were causing me all kinds of problems. He gave me enzymes for them, I'm not sure they are working so well though."

Okay then, I marveled keeping my thoughts to myself, we were going, unannounced, in the evening, when it was most likely family time, to visit Benny Zook hoping he could do some more tests on Samuel and possibly suggest more natural supplements to cure the problem. Rolling my eyes and shaking my head, I did as I told. I knew Benny Zook quite well as I'd brought several Amish to his home for treatments. Since the Amish communities were, for the most part, independent of the rest of society, several Amish communities had people that fulfilled different roles that would otherwise be filled by professionals in the Englischer communities. For example, the Amish often had their own midwives. A lesser-known fact was that in a few communities there are also people known as healers whom the community members went to for assistance with ailments. Most of those healers were self-taught though a few had studied and obtained certifications so they were legally licensed to draw blood and take urine samples.

Benny welcomed Samuel into his office, checked his blood and discovered there were indeed still parasites in it. He gave Samuel more suggestions to rid himself of them. With Samuel satisfied, we were off once again, but where to?

■　■　■

"Haley, do you know those German Baptists," Samuel piped up from the back seat?

"No, I don't know anything about German Baptists," I responded, "except for the ones I've seen in Dalton pulling out teeth."

"I'd like to stop in and talk to the one that owns the harness shop and see if he wants to purchase any of my cream separators. You know, I have quite a thriving cream separator sales business going on, lots of customers."

Toby, the only levelheaded one of the bunch, thankfully could direct me to the German Baptist community; outside of Salina, Missouri, a place I'd never been to. The fact that the sun still shone made it easier to navigate the unfamiliar winding roads, rolling hills, forests and pastures to the middle of nowhere. Upon arriving in the community, Samuel, believing he knew where he was going, instructed Toby to direct me to a house down a long lane. I'd never been to a German Baptist house and there I was, at supper time, driving in unannounced with three men. I was a little nervous not knowing anything about the German Baptists, except for the fact they wanted to be left alone to live their lives in their own tight knit community. Yet, there I was, a total stranger, bringing total strangers to their front door. We stopped in front of the simple two-story brown wood siding house, with wrap around porch. The three men knocked on the door only to discover that was not the house Samuel was looking for. Getting back in the van, with a jolly voice Samuel quipped, "I think he was interested in my cream separators. I might have just gained another customer."

Toby, the respectful man that he was, politely responded, "That's wonderful Samuel. You are quite the businessman." With that, we were off again expecting the next house, per the directions of the German

Baptist man we'd just so rudely intruded upon, would be the correct one." I pulled down a narrow gravel lane ending at the driveway of a German Baptist home where lights were on, as darkness had fallen by then. A buggy full of visitors had just arrived as well. My three unusual passengers approached the house, knocked on the door and were invited into the home. About twenty minutes later, during which time I got a lot of crocheting done, a silent Abe, distressed looking Toby who had the look of wondering what was going on and why was he a part of it, and cheerful Samuel returned. Samuel apparently had gotten whatever it was he came after; he had gained another customer.

Continuing the adventure, I listened for my next clue, which Samuel promptly gave, offering; "now Toby, I may have left a few thank you gifts in your home from my stay. I had several combs, the kind that are plastic, thin, with no handles that you can purchase by the bagful at Wal-Mart or another such discount store. You see, I'm missing a few and I like to have a lot on hand."

I suggested that when we got to Joseph we stop at the Dollar Tree as they might have what he was looking for. Samuel agreed; and they did. By then we'd traveled for a few hours and the whole trip Abe sat there looking forward without saying a word or indicating that he'd heard any of the conversation going on around him. Meanwhile, Samuel, once again was sitting behind me droning on and on and on about his combs, his big plans to sell cream separators to his long list of clients if only he could get a hold of cream separators and about a hand full of people that still owed him a dollar. "Hmm," he reflected half to himself, "I'd like to take a trip to him and see if I can collect on that dollar."

■ ■ ■

"Next stop," announced a relieved Toby "is Robertsville where we will drop off Samuel." During the hour trip there, Samuel droned on about his adventures in visiting forty-three different Amish communities in the states of Wisconsin, Iowa, Missouri, Illinois, Indiana and Ohio over the past three months; and again, how he had lost his wife in June. I listened intently, "She was a large woman," he offered. "She had an enlarged heart which eventually led to her demise. She wasn't able to have children for years, not until her forties, and then she was only able to have two, a boy and a girl. Clements, our boy, is very large, well past six feet tall. He saw fit to leave the Amish church and go work with people overseas. I don't understand why he can't work with people here. I'm not in agreement with what he's doing."

Keeping the conversation going because I was tired and needed to stay awake, I inquired about his daughter.

"Her, oh, she's in her late twenties and married with four young children. She remained Amish."

"Will you be staying with her over Christmas," I wanted to know?

"Probably not; I don't know where I'll be for Christmas."

"You know Samuel, you have so many interesting adventures and stories, have you ever thought about writing a book?"

"I suppose I could, but probably not." He answered.

Our conversation of small talk continued among the three of us, as Abe just sat, still not participating, though obviously enjoying the ride. I believed he listened closely to every word that was said.

I wasn't sure who decided where we would deposit Samuel, but in Robertsville we found a family that welcomed him. Once Samuel was settled in his forty-fourth community, Toby almost shyly asked me if, since we were in Robertsville, his former hometown, we could drop by his old property and collect some items, then stop at the furniture makers and pick up two rocking chairs for his daughter's Christmas gifts. "Of course," I answered. "I'm happy to help with Christmas shopping," adding, "and please, always ask me anything. I'm happy to do what I can whenever I can." With that we ran his errands then headed home.

Abe, still quiet in the front seat, surprised me by leaning close to my ear and asking a question. "So, what is your name?" I didn't realize he could speak or hear. Well, wonders never cease. What an interesting and memorable night for all of us.

"You can preach a better sermon with your life than with your lips." — *Amish Proverb*

Our accommodation in the Amish home

26

Salt and Pepper

The early spring day my husband Allen and I took the Amish work crew, Allen drove and worked for, to a horse auction in Centerville, Iowa was like a feather in the wind. Illustrative of how the Amish often operated, their minds were all over the place and so were the places we drove them. As usual, nothing went according to plan, if there ever was a plan. Our responsibility as drivers, they believed, was to go with anything they decided upon at any moment, and with a smile.

We picked up our first passenger as scheduled at 6:00 a.m. After picking him up, we made our rounds to gather the rest of our passengers. Communication about the event was rough, as some Amish who'd originally decided to go changed their minds while others, at the last minute decided to go. We drove all over the community adding to the trip needless miles and time.

While traveling to the horse auction, Vernon piped up from the second bench back. "Why you see those headlights on that vehicle? He must have been talking about a woman."

Allen glanced at Vernon in his rear-view mirror trying to figure out what Vernon meant by that cryptic message. Finally, he understood that Vernon wanted the radio turned on. Next Vernon piped up about some guy named Waylon who was his neighbor and he wondered how Waylon was doing. Allen turned to me motioning to the CD pouch for the Waylon Jennings CD. I had no idea who Waylon Jennings was, but I obeyed. Next Vernon waved his hand, which Allen interpreted as "turn up the music" so Allen turned up the music to a level I wouldn't have ever had it at; and I like to listen to loud music.

Vernon felt he couldn't directly ask for music to be turned on or turned up due to the strict belief system he was raised with, the idea that music was only for the worship of God and should bring one closer to Him. On the other hand, if the driver were to turn on the radio while Amish were along that would be acceptable. So, he cleverly made up a code to communicate his desires to Allen. I was completely baffled, but Allen seemed to understand.

Everybody in the van except for me had attended several horse auctions. For many of the Amish, it was a form of entertainment as well as a social event. Pulling into the parking lot, we had a hard time finding a spot as there were seemingly endless numbers of large vans and trucks with attached horse trailers. Parked, Allen led me to an outdoor oval shaped dirt track. There dozens of mostly Amish men in their black shoes, black slacks, black coats, and black hats stood watching majestic, spirited horses. Heads held high; their powerful legs carried them effortlessly around the track. Tails floating like lustrous streamers in their wake, the clippity clop of their hooves tossed dust into the cool March air.

Behind them, black steel wheeled chariots occupied by Amish drivers carrying whips and hair blowing in the wind, swiftly sped around the track. I'd never seen such a thing. Allen explained that racing was one way for the auction attendees to get an idea of the horses available and to see their beauty and abilities. The actual auction would be held inside the stadium, one horse at a time.

Our Amish very much enjoyed their day at the horse auction just watching and visiting with friends from other Amish communities, having no desire to purchase a horse.

After the all-day event, we headed back first making a stop at a popular western store in one of Iowa's many small towns. After that we hurried to get to the bank by 4:30 p.m. so David A could cash a check. We were late. The bank had closed, but the drive-thru was open so he walked through it. What a funny man.

Back in the community, we dropped off our passengers with the expectation that they'd ready themselves and we'd return shortly to take them out to eat. Allen and I had to pick up a stock trailer from a non-Amish man and deliver it to Herman, whom I would be driving the next day. He'd requested it be delivered to his house that evening so that he could load it by morning for our trip. Allen and I stopped by Cody's, Herman's friend, hooked the trailer on the van, made a stop to invite another Amish man to dinner that evening, then dropped off the trailer at Herman's house.

Just as Allen was backing it down his lane, out came Herman looking like a red haired, white skinned sumo wrestler, except that he was fully clothed. He had difficulty walking, not only due to his excess weight, but also due to a medical condition of his feet. "Well, it turns out Cody needs his trailer tonight, so I need you to return the trailer where you got it," he stated. Allen and I looked at each other thinking the same thing, 'Feather in the wind.' Sighing, we did as he requested.

With the Trailer dropped off at Cody's, we made the rounds to pick up Allen's work crew and their wives, whom he was treating to dinner in a neighboring town that evening. After picking up Billy, Nettie, Eli and Lydia, Lamar, Katie and the rest of the crew and their ladies, Allen noticed his van was out of fuel and would not make it to the next town. So, like a feather in the wind, Allen's fault that time, we had to drive out of the way to fuel up before heading to our destination.

Finally, an hour and a half later than we should have, we made it to the barbeque restaurant in Zig Zag. The waitress pushed a few tables together so we could sit down and eat as a group.

One idea I had about the Amish before getting to know them was that they were backward, boring, and bashful. Not so. Many of them were quite the opposite. They were big hearted, blithe and bright. The food was scrumptious, the company delightful, and the conversation enlightening. After discussing news and local happenings, followed by some curious dirty talk by the Amish at the dinner table involving bread and exercise, not to mention ice being thrown down people's shirts, including mine, Vernon decided it was time to visit Allen's mother's house to see her 8,000 plus sets of salt and pepper shakers.

While on route to the restaurant, Allen received a call from Herman. "Oh, you know Cody doesn't need to haul his horse tonight after all so I shouldn't have had you return the trailer. Will you please go pick up the trailer at Cody's and bring it back to my house tonight?"

"Why sure buddy," Allen politely responded. Feather in the wind... "Can you do that by eight?" Herman wanted to know.

We didn't leave the restaurant until eight and had yet to drive twenty-two miles to visit Allen's mother first. Carol, an elderly sagacious woman, fragile, with short white hair graciously greeted us at her front door. She'd never had Amish in her home before, so their visit was as interesting to her as being in her home was to them. Making themselves comfortable, the women and children sat on the couch in the living room while the men nosed around taking note of the many family photos displayed on shelves and walls. Carol followed them around answering their questions. Seeing pictures of a much younger Allen, innocent looking, thin, longer blond hair, they joked, "He looks like Eli. He looks Amish." Eli was one of the young men on the work crew.

■　■　■

The salt and pepper collection tour began upstairs where Carol kept hundreds of sets on shelves and in cabinets. She then lead us downstairs to a large room that was literally lined wall to wall, top to bottom with bookshelves covered in thousands of salt and pepper shaker sets. They were organized according to category— fruits and vegetables, buildings, Disney figures, sea animals, people, wooden shakers, kitchen themed shakers, cat shakers, state shakers, religious shakers, plant shakers etc. You name it, she had it. They loved the salt and pepper shakers. Allen, Carol and I enjoyed watching the Amish as much as the Amish enjoyed looking at the shakers.

Nettie, an attractive auburn haired, freckle-faced bold girl of nineteen, was fascinated with the more unsavory salt and pepper shakers. She got quite a kick out of them. "Haley, come here," she called to me, handheld to her mouth, trying to be inconspicuous. I came and she pointed to salt and pepper shaker female legs and laughing, she said, "Haley, those are your legs."

"Why thank you Nettie, those are quite attractive legs, what a compliment," I joked with her. My stars, I thought, I hope she's not looking that closely at my body.

Then she discovered a cute, fat little girl and boy set. "Hey Haley, I found you and Allen. Look," She pointed mischievously. She and her boyfriend, Billy, continued looking at shakers.

After about a half hour stay, we loaded up and returned our Amish to their homes, first dropping off Lamar and Katie. Next, we returned to Cody's house to pick up the trailer and then Allen dropped me off at Rufus and Levi's house so I could talk to them. They had called twice during the day wanting me to take them to Canada and I had no cell service. Allen continued on to the other's homes and finally deposited the trailer at Herman's again. By the time we dropped off our final passengers, it was 9:30 p.m., a late night.

We still had much to do. Clean and fill Allen's van, stop at his mom's again, prepare his van so he could drive the work crew the next morning, prepare my van for hauling the trailer, and finally we had to pack snacks for the next day. Everything accomplished, exhausted, we finally headed to bed at midnight. Up at 5:00 a.m., we rushed to get ready unable to even get a bite for breakfast before leaving the house because we had to be at our locations at 6:00 a.m. By the time we arrived at the homes, our stomachs ached with hunger pains. That was the life of an Amish Driver. It was frantic, unpredictable and not at all glamorous, but so rewarding.

■ ■ ■

Afterward: The Amish were like feathers in the wind. You just never knew what they'd come up with. In fact, Herman had instructed me the night before to pick up David J at 6:00 a.m. He swore that he'd Tales of Driving the Amish 175 told David J that I'd be there at 6:00 a.m., so I arrived at 6:00 a.m. David, his wife and infant daughter were not ready to leave until 6:25 a.m., which meant I could have slept in another half an hour. We got to Herman's after 6:30. The work crew had agreed to help Herman load his buggy into my horse trailer for the trip to Yachats. Well, the work crew was loaded and on their way to Iowa by the time we got to Herman's because of all those miscommunications. Things worked out though, they always did with a little bit of patience, optimism and kindness; a feather in the wind.

"Days are like suitcases, all the same size, but some people are able to pack more into them than others." —*Amish Proverb*

Salt and pepper shaker collection in an Amish home

Library in an Amish home

For Further Information

20 most asked questions about the Amish and Mennonites – Meryl and Phyllis Good

Amish Society – John A. Hostetler

Behind the Blue Curtains – Lizzy Hershberger

History of the Amish: Revised and Updated – Steven M. Nolt

Living without electricity – Stephen Scott and Kenneth Pellman

Martyrs Mirror – Thieleman J. Van Braght

Our People: The Amish and Mennonites of Ohio – Levi Miller

The puzzle of Amish Life – Donald B Kraybill

What it is like to be Amish - Sam S. Stoltzfus

Why do they dress that way? - Stephen Scott

Old order buggy in Minnesota

Upcoming Book Two

Amish Christmas Mishaps

When Haley and Alan drive the Amish north for Christmas, they don't know what they're getting themselves into. Their trip takes a dangerous turn when an unexpected blizzard sweeps across the Midwest. With snow and ice mounting, temperatures plummeting, and danger at every turn, they must rely on their faith, resilience, and the kindness of strangers for survival. Amidst the peril, heartwarming miracles unfold in the most surprising ways, reminding everyone of the true meaning of Christmas.

About the Author

Haley Straw (pictured above with her six children) is a native of Portland, Oregon in the United States of America. She now lives surrounded by her Amish friends in rural Missouri on a ten-acre farm. She's a hippy, home-schooling mama to six, and a green smoothie drinking chocolate addict. In her rare spare moments, she enjoys writing, teaching, speaking, crocheting and being outdoors.

Let's stay in touch!
You can find all my social media links, updates and extras at
www.HaleyStraw.com

www.ingramcontent.com/pod-product-compliance
Lightning Source LLC
Chambersburg PA
CBHW021150130626
46554CB00005B/1748